Medieval Fare

Medieval Fare

Food and Culture in Medieval Iberia

Martha M. Daas

LEXINGTON BOOKS
Lanham • Boulder • New York • London

Published by Lexington Books
An imprint of The Rowman & Littlefield Publishing Group, Inc.
4501 Forbes Boulevard, Suite 200, Lanham, Maryland 20706
www.rowman.com

86-90 Paul Street, London EC2A 4NE

British Library Cataloguing in Publication Information Available

Library of Congress Cataloging-in-Publication Data

Names: Daas, Martha Mary, author.
Title: Medieval fare : food and culture in medieval Iberia / Martha M. Daas.
Description: Lanham, Maryland : Lexington Books, [2022] |
   Includes bibliographical references and index.
Identifiers: LCCN 2022031451 (print) | LCCN 2022031452 (ebook) |
   ISBN 9781498589598 (Cloth) | ISBN 9781498589604 (eBook) Subjects: LCSH:
Food habits—Iberian Peninsula—History—To 1500. Classification: LCC
GT2853.I16 D33 2022 (print) | LCC GT2853.I16 (ebook) |
   DDC 394.1/2—dc23/eng/20220715
LC record available at https://lccn.loc.gov/2022031451
LC ebook record available at https://lccn.loc.gov/2022031452

Contents

Introduction

Medieval Iberia was not one unified country nor was it known by one name. Muslims called their home *al-Andalus*; Jews called it *Sefarad*, and Christians used the Latin *Hispania*. Throughout this book, I will refer to this land as Iberia. Unique in its cultural and religious makeup, medieval Iberia represented a kind of crossroads of cultures. This crossroads was reflected on both large and small scales. On the grand scale, there was a sharing of intellectual ideas and new ideas of how best to survive, including great innovations in agriculture and science. On a more intimate level, the habits of daily life often intersected among members of the three religions. The acts of producing, cooking, and eating demonstrate the political realities of the land: at times interdependent, and, at times, at odds. Political domination varied throughout the centuries but ended with Christian conquest and rule. This book is an investigation of the cultural complexity of medieval Iberia before 1500 as it is revealed through references to food and habits of production and consumption.

There are a variety of texts through which we can begin to understand how people lived and what they ate. By examining food manuals, health treatises, religious and literary texts, a picture begins to form. Access to food, both in its variety and its quantity, depended on a number of factors: whether one owned land or was a tenant farmer, whether one was part of a thriving religious order, whether one came from the aristocracy or the working poor, and so on.

If a person or family was fortunate enough to own a small patch of land, this land had something planted on it, like grapevines, vegetable gardens, and/or fruit trees. All three religions practiced transhumance, moving livestock according to the season. Grazing rights became important legal battles in the Middle Ages, as the union of sheepherders gained political power throughout the Christian conquest of the peninsula.[1]

Markets thrived in medieval Iberia. Every city, every town catered to its population with daily and weekly markets. Under Muslim rule, *hisba* manuals demonstrated the strict regulations that governed all aspects of the sale of food: from price regulations to cleanliness. These manuals were created above all to avoid fraud in the marketplace.[2] Under Christian rule, market regulations, influenced by the *hisba* manuals, were put into place in the fifteenth century. Permanent stalls were set up as were small shops that catered to specific tastes. Roving fruit and vegetable sellers existed, but prices were still fixed by regulators.[3]

In cities, women baked their bread in communal ovens. The business of flour was strictly controlled, as wheat shortages were common. James Anderson writes that "a rise in the cost of bread could lead to riots."[4] Most people could not afford wheat and relied on barley or rye for their daily bread. Wheat was the most prized flour, but only the wealthy, and the Church, could afford it on a daily basis. Aside from certain food taboos, most people, whether Christian, Muslim or Jewish, ate a similar diet, based on their economic status. Poorer people made do with legumes, vegetables, dairy products, and lower-quality bread. Wealthier people had a steady diet of a variety of meats, cheeses, and other delicacies.

The midday meal was the largest in the Middle Ages. Those who worked ate around 1:00 p.m. and returned to work after the meal. Wealthier people ate later, had multiple courses, and napped after the meal.[5] The poor had little access to meat, while the middle class would have had one slice of goat or lamb per meal, about fifty grams per person. For the aristocracy, on the other hand, 350 grams per person would be the norm.[6]

The difference in consumption between the wealthy and the poor was more profound than anything we can imagine today. C. M. Woolgar gives an example of the household of Marie d'Anjou, Queen of Majorca. In the year 1340–1341, her household spent 243 pounds on foodstuffs:

> 68 pounds on wheat (for bread); 55 on wine; 52 on mutton, pork and veal, fat and rabbits, 19 on poultry, pigeons and partridges, 13 on fish (only tuna is named), 9 on spices (cinnamon, cloves, pepper, saffron, mustard, vinegar, sugar and honey), 7 on eggs, 7 on fresh and dried vegetables (cabbage, leeks, spinach, root veg, gourds, onions, garlic, chickpeas, beans, lentils), 5 on salt and oil, 4 on fresh and dried fruit (almond, cherries, chestnuts, figs, peaches, filberts and nuts, pomegranates), 4 on cheeses and 2 on sauces and condiments including oranges as a sauce.[7]

A poorer household would have little to no access to wheat and would rely on legumes, dairy, and eggs for its main sources of protein. If one lived near a river, however, fresh fish would be available throughout the year.

The calendar was marked by both feasting and fasting. Fasting was a common practice in the Middle Ages. For Christians, there were at least two fast days a week plus the forty days of Lent. These fast days required Christians to eat meatless meals, so fish and legumes were often on the menu. Jews and Muslims also fasted during religious holidays but were less prescribed in their intake of foods during those periods (except for Passover). Feasts centered on religious holidays, the end of fasting periods, and, for the wealthy, banquets.

FOOD AND HEALTH MANUALS

We are fortunate to have a number of food and health manuals from the Middle Ages that give us a window into the world of eating. Muslim, Jewish, and Christian scholars wrote a number of treatises that address food and health. These medical men followed in the footsteps of Greek, Latin, Jewish, Arab, and Persian scholars on health. Quoting from Dioscorides, Ibn Sina, Galen, and others, there is, unsurprisingly, a number of similarities in the approaches to healthy eating. The association of foodstuffs with corresponding humoral categories is the basis of most healthy food regimens in the Middle Ages. The humoral theory states that all foods can be categorized by their inherent nature: cold, warm, hot, wet, damp, or dry. Every person can be categorized by their nature: sanguine, melancholic, choleric, or phlegmatic. The goal was simply to find a balance between one's nature and the food that one ate. If, for example, a person was sanguine by nature (which would be associated with passion, joviality, and excess), then to cool one's temperament, a physician would prescribe foods that were known for their cool and wet properties.

One text written around 1418 or 1419 titled *Sevillana medicina* lays out quite explicitly the daily diet one should follow living in warmer climates. The author, Juan de Aviñón, writes that a healthy person should eat approximately four pounds of food a day, one of which should be bread. The others consist of wine, meat, and other foodstuffs that he does not specify. He does mention, however, that wine should be drunk rather than water, because water "non da nudrimento"[8] (does not provide nourishment), according to doctors of the time.[9]

The most comprehensive and influential book on dietetics written by a Christian was the *Régimen de salud*, by Arnaldo de Vilanova. Vilanova was the personal physician to Jaime II of Aragón. This exhaustive text, written in 1307, covered health, eating, and hygiene. It became one of the most influential medical texts of the Middle Ages. This text outlines the humoral qualities of all foodstuffs as well as human temperaments and even goes as far as assigning temperaments to specific zodiac signs.

Born in Córdoba in the twelfth century, the great scholar Abū al-Walīd
M. b. Ahmad b. M. b. Rušd, known as Ibn Rushd or by the Latinized name
Averroes, is famous for a number of treatises on medicine, science, and phi-
losophy. His medical book known in Latin as the *Colliget* was one of the most
influential texts throughout the Middle Ages and the early modern periods
(see figure 0.1). This book gives detailed recommendations about the quantity
and frequency of meals, the order in which different foods should be ingested,
and the changes in diet with age and build.[10]

Moses b. 'Abd Allāh b. Maimūn al-Qurtabī al Isra'īlī, known as Maimonides (1135–1204), wrote a treatise also titled *El régimen de la salud* at
the end of the twelfth century for the Sultan al-Malik al Afdal, who was the
son of Saladin. This text, according to Gerrit Bos, was one that enjoyed great
popularity among Jewish populations throughout the Middle East and in
Italy, where it was one of the first texts on medicine recommended to Hebrew
scholars.[11]

Along with health treatises are a number of food manuals written between
the thirteenth and fifteenth centuries. We have examples of both Muslim and

Figure 0.1   Title page from a Latin edition of *Colliget*, Averroes's main work in medicine, 1530.

Christian cookbooks. Although no extant Jewish cookbook exists, David Gitlitz and Linda Kay Davidson unearthed a number of recipes from Jewish households through Inquisition transcripts and eyewitness accounts. The earliest text we have is Ibn Razīn's *Fudālat al-hiwān fī tayyībāt al-ta'ām wa-l-alwān* (*Relieves de las mesas, acerca de las delicias de la comida y los diferentes platos*) from the thirteenth century. Manuela Marín, editor of this cookbook, writes that this text never appeared in any bibliographic notation about the author and is, ironically, the only one of his texts that has survived.[12] Although the author lived an expatriate life in Tunis and Ceuta, his work reflects the foods of *al-Andalus*. This incredible resource, which has been preserved in two extant manuscripts, contains over four hundred recipes divided into a number of sections. The first one contains the most recipes (ninety-seven) and is devoted entirely to grains and desserts. The next longest section is the one on meat, with ninety recipes. Poultry takes up seventy recipes, fish and eggs forty-one. Other sections include vegetables, legumes, dairy, preserves, sweets, and, at the end, powders and soaps.

The anonymous Catalan cookbook *The Book of Sent Sovi* is the earliest Christian cookbook available to us, written in the fourteenth century and preserved in one extant manuscript from the fifteenth century. This manuscript contains seventy-two recipes that include a number of sauces, porridge, stews, vegetable dishes, custards, and fritters. Since the recipes did not provide step-by-step instructions, it is assumed that the book was intended for culinary professionals who used it more as a reference guide. Many of the recipes would be difficult to follow for the average home cook, and many were intended for banquets.[13]

Mestre Ruperto de Nola's *Libre de coch (libro de cozina)* is the first cookbook published in Spain (in 1520), although it was written much earlier (see figure 0.2). Carolyn Nadeau writes that the text was translated into Castilian in 1525 and published eleven times in less than fifty years.[14] This text contains not only recipes for the wealthy table but also a whole section on Lenten cuisine. The introductory chapters deal with dietary health, carving, and serving at table.

The *Manual de mugeres en el qual se contienen muchas y diversas reçeutas muy buenas* is an anonymous text written in the late fifteenth century that details advice for women in the areas of dietetics, cosmetics, cooking, and hygiene. The burgeoning middle class called for a kind of new domestic bliss. Women were being asked to stay home and play a particular role.[15] Women were expected to know how to sew, cook, prepare perfumes, and have a notion of domestic medicine.[16] The *Manual de mugeres* is an amalgam of cookbooks, domestic manuals, and medical handbooks. In this text, we see how women used spices, wine, dried fruits and nuts, and other expensive items to create a variety of perfumes, balsams, creams, soaps, medicines, and, of course, recipes, although cooking is not the main concern of the book. Out

Figure 0.2 Title page of the *Libre de doctrina pera ben Seruir: De Tallar y del Art de Coch* (1520), Roberto de Nola.

of 145 recipes, only 29 were specifically for food.[17] This leaves a large number of mixtures that were targeted for health and well-being left in the capable hands of women. This text offers some insight into the role of women in healing in Spain.

Jewish cooking traditions are outlined in Gitlitz and Davidson's *A Drizzle of Honey*. The collection of recipes, gleaned from Inquisition trial testimonies, range from the years 1450–1677. The authors write that more than half of these testimonies are from eyewitness accounts.[18] The variety of recipes demonstrates the relative wealth of the households, as the liberal use of sugar, spices, and meat are showcased. Like the Muslim food manuals, lamb, fowl, and beef are featured, as well as eggs and dairy. The section on holiday foods, with its focus on Jewish holidays, and the noted absence of pork and shellfish, mark the recipes as traditionally Jewish or crypto-Jewish.

AGRICULTURAL MANUALS

Agricultural treatises provide a rich source of information on the kinds of foods that were planted and the advances in agriculture brought to Iberia by the Muslims (see figure 0.3). The *Tratado de agricultura* is an agricultural calendar written by 'Abd al-Rahmān ibn Muhammad ibn Wāfid, in the eleventh century. This text details agricultural activities that took place month to month. The tenth-century *Calendario de Córdoba*, is most often attributed to the Mozarab bishop Recemundo, also known as Rabbi ibn Zyad. According to Eduardo Cerrato Casado, however, the *Calendario* may be a combination of two works: the aforementioned work by Bishop Recemundo and also the *Kitab al-anwā*, translated into Latin as the *Liber annoe*, attributed to Arib ibn Sa'id.[19] The *Calendario* outlines what should be planted and harvested each month. Along with this prosaic information, the author includes meteorological observations, the signs of the Zodiac, recommendations on the best food and drink to eat each month, and holidays.

LITERARY TEXTS

There are a variety of ways in which the cultural complexity of medieval Iberia is revealed through references to food and consumption. Aside from the medical texts, agricultural treatises, and cookbooks, literary texts can also

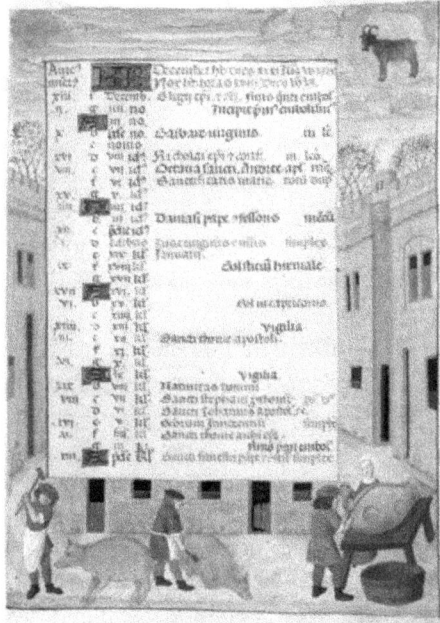

Figure 0.3 A calendar page for December, with illuminated initials "KL," and an illustrated border with the symbol of Capricorn as a goat. Below is a landscape of people slaughtering pigs, cooking them on a fire, and butchering them. *Source*: Netherlands, S. Bruges.

give us a sense of what people might have eaten. Although literature is not necessarily an accurate method by which we can understand the past, there is no doubt that we are able to use references to food and consumption in order to gain a greater understanding of daily habits and common foods. Food references can also give us an insight into folklore, prejudices, and fear.

In this book, the texts that will be examined were originally written in Castilian, Catalan, Hebrew, and Arabic. Most versions are translated into either Castilian or English. The main Castilian texts used in this book are Gonzalo de Berceo's thirteenth-century collection of miracle tales titled *Milagros de Nuestra Señora* (*The Miracles of Our Lady*) and Juan Ruiz's fourteenth-century *Libro de buen amor* (*The Book of Good Love*). Other Castilian texts that make an appearance are the fifteenth-century collection of poems titled *Cancionera de Baena* and the smaller collection that was found originally within the *Baena* collection, the *Cancionero de burlas provocantes de risa*. Certain hagiographical texts, including the thirteenth-century *Lives of Saint Mary the Egyptian and Saint Martha*, are also referenced. The Hebrew texts cited in this book are the English translations by Raymond Scheindlin in his anthology *Wine, Women, and Death*, David Simha Segal's translation of Judah al-Harizi's *Book of Tahkemoni*, and Peter Cole's anthology *The Dream of the Poem: Hebrew Poetry from Muslim and Christian Spain*. For Arabic poetry, James T. Monroe's anthology titled *Hispano-Arabic Poetry* and Corriente Córdoba's *El cancionero hispanoárabe* are cited.

Gonzalo de Berceo was a thirteenth-century cleric who wrote a number of texts celebrating the lives of the saints and the Virgin Mary. His collection of miracle tales titled *Milagros de Nuestra Señora* is, arguably, his most famous text. The collection includes twenty-five tales or *exempla* preceded by an allegorical introduction. Food references in this collection tend toward the spiritual, focusing mainly on food metaphors of Christ and Mary and foods as metaphors for virtue or vice.

Libro de buen amor is a fourteenth-century text written by an author who uses the pseudonym Juan Ruiz, Archpriest of Hita. The main plot of the text is an accounting of the author's love affairs, interspersed with fables, morality tales, *exempla*, poems, and hymns dedicated to the Virgin Mary. Through this wild array of narratives, the reader is witness to a number of scenes in which food plays an incredibly important role. One of these scenes is the iconic battle between Lord Carnal and Lady Lent, which is discussed at length in chapter 1, dedicated to meats and mains (see figure 0.4). Other food references appear in parodic scenes of enticement and love making as well as commentary on the agricultural calendar.

Scheindlin's anthology gives us an in-depth view of the world of wine parties. Wine parties took place in both Muslim and Jewish households. After dinner, both Muslim and Jewish revelers sat around on cushions drinking wine, enjoying entertainment, and entering into poetic contests and spirited

Figure 0.4 *The Fight Between Carnival and Lent* (1559), by Pieter Bruegel the Elder.

debate. Much of the politics and mores of the time can be gleaned from both Hebrew and Arabic traditions of wine poetry.

In al-Harizi's *Tahkemoni* there are a number of stories that highlight the food of medieval Iberia as well as warning against gluttonous consumption and displays of drunkenness. In gate 3, the metaphorical banquet and the glutton's consumption of that banquet represent the golden age of Hebrew poetry in Iberia. In gate 27, there is a poetic challenge between the woes and joys of drinking. As in *Libro de buen amor,* there is tension between religious abstention and worldly joys.[20] In the poems relating to food in Peter Cole's anthology, food most often is used as metaphor for love but also bitterness and betrayal.

In the Arabic poems translated by James T. Monroe, times of joy and times of sorrow are marked with poetry about food and drink. The twelfth-century Cordoban poet Ibn Quzmān waxes poetic about food, but most often about wine. As an observer of the Almoravid society, Ibn Quzmān's poetry demonstrates the gap between what was dictated by law and what was practiced by the people.

CHAPTER ORGANIZATION

The book is divided into chapters focusing on particular foodstuffs. Chapter 1 focuses on meats and other sources of protein, including dairy and eggs. The kinds of meats and proteins and the amounts that people ate were affected both by religion and by economics. Pigs were easy and inexpensive to maintain, so most Christian households with any means had at least one. Hens kept for eggs were also common in households of all three religions. Manuela Marín writes that the number of eggs required in many of the recipes in *Relieves de las mesas* is more proof that the book was written for the aristocratic diet, since no middle-class household could afford to be so liberal.[21] Dairy was consumed in the form of cheese and made mainly from the milk of sheep and goats. However, fresh milk is called for in a few recipes found in *Relieves de las mesas*, cooked into certain stews and also for rice pudding.

The popularity of sheepherding exploded among Muslims and Christians in the Middle Ages. Unlike pigs, sheep could be used in their entirety. Glick writes that early in the Middle Ages, sheep were raised for meat. However, Christians later considered the wool to be the most valuable aspect of the animal.[22]

Pork was the main marker of the Christian diet. In the fifteenth century, abstention from pork was suspicious enough to be reported to the inquisitors. Although Jews and Muslims were allowed to buy meat from their own butchers, converts were required to buy meat from Christian butchers.[23]

Chapter 2 investigates the topic of breads and grains. Bread was the single most important element of the medieval diet. Poorer people relied on bread to provide them with enough sustenance to get through their workday. Most people ate a pound to a pound and a half of bread per day.

The kinds of flours and grains that people consumed were affected both by religion and by economics. Wheat was considered the finest of grains. Most poor people could go their entire lives without ever having tasted wheat bread except during their annual or semi-annual communion. Christian law stated that the host must only be made with wheat flour.[24] Most people ate bread made of barley or rye, grains that were considered almost as good as wheat. Oats were considered to be animal fodder.[25]

Rice, pasta, and couscous made their way into the households of all three religions. Couscous became known as a Muslim grain and therefore was not as popular at Christian tables.[26] Rice, originally considered an exotic grain, became one of the most common staples in the medieval diet as did different types of pasta.[27]

Chapter 3 focuses on vegetables and legumes. Muslim and Jewish diets relied more heavily on vegetables and legumes, which is the reason for the large number of vegetable-heavy recipes in both *Relieves* and *A Drizzle of Honey*. By the fifteenth century, certain vegetables were considered non-Christian, especially eggplants, chard, and, in the legume category, chickpeas.[28]

Herbs were used in abundance in the recipes of all three religions. Often, recipes simply called for "all the good herbs." Herbs are common both in cooking manuals and in health handbooks. The *Manual de mugeres*, for example, discusses herbs in the context of homemade cosmetics and tinctures. Only a few spices were native to Spain, the rest coming from the East. Most spices were financially out of reach for poorer households. However, according to Vilanova, spices were dangerous for lower classes except for pepper, which was both affordable and "suitable for rustics."[29]

Fruits and sweets are the topics of chapter 4. The agricultural innovations brought to medieval Spain by Arabs caused an explosion of available fruits. Christian farmers in northern Iberia focused their efforts on hearty fruit trees like apples, pears, and cherries. Glick writes that the grapevine was also a "cornerstone of Christian agricultural expansion."[30] Figs, introduced by Arabs, became one of the most popular crops in medieval Iberia.[31] Dried fruits were a delicacy and often served as dessert. Nuts were a common and essential form of protein. Almond milk replaced dairy in many recipes, especially during Lent. Sugar cane was introduced to the Iberian Peninsula in the twelfth century, but it was not until the fifteenth century that sugar cane became a widely produced crop, especially in Andalucía and the areas surrounding Valencia. Sugar was always expensive and therefore out of reach for many medieval people.[32] Honey, however, was widely available and easily obtained.

The final chapter of the book focuses on wine. Wine holds a special place in the cultures of medieval Iberia. Wine, according to medieval medical professionals, is both food and medicine. Everyone, from small children to aging monks, drank wine daily, although often watered or spiced. Grapes were one of the most common crops grown by Muslims, Christians, and Jews. Often, households would grow grapevines for personal use on small plots of land. Although drinking wine was prohibited by the Qur'an, there is much evidence that points to laxity in that area of religious practice. Next to bread, wine was the most important element of the medieval diet. Glick writes that Benedictine rule "specified that monks should drink one liter of wine per day."[33] A family could easily consume three liters of wine per day.[34]

Although it is easy to focus on the differences in the habits of consumption, it is more likely that these distinctions were less obvious to those living through the Middle Ages. Brian Catlos writes that the boundaries that were intended to divide the communities were often blurred or even erased.[35] By examining a wide range of texts—including literature, cooking and health manuals, and "official" documents—today's reader will be able to begin to understand both the segregative nature and the acculturated tastes of medieval Iberia. Whether we call it *al-Andalus*, *Sefarad*, or *Hispania*, this land produced cultures of consumption that both reflect an interdependence of cultures and demonstrate a prohibition of commensality based on religion.

NOTES

1. Teófilo Ruiz, *Crisis and Continuity: Land and Town in Late Medieval Castile* (Philadelphia: University of Philadelphia Press, 1994), 91.

2. Fernando Hidalgo, Jesús D. Lopez-Manjón, and Francisco Carrasco Fenech, "Cost Calculations, Religion, and Commerce: The Book of Good Government of the Souk of Málaga in the 13th Century," Working Paper (Seville: Universidad Pablo de Olavide, Department of Business Administration, 2009), 21.

3. Tomás Puñal Fernández, *El Mercado en Madrid en la Baja Edad Media* (Madrid: Caja de Madrid, 1992), 240.

4. James Anderson, *Daily Life during the Spanish Inquisition* (Westport: Greenwood Press, 2002), 187.

5. Anderson, *Daily Life during the Spanish Inquisition*, 184–85.

6. Anderson, *Daily Life during the Spanish Inquisition*, 187.

7. C. M. Woolgar, "Food and Taste in Europe in the Middle Ages," in *Food: The History of Taste,* ed. Paul Freedman (London: Thames & Hudson, 2007), 181.

8. Juan de Aviñon, *Sevillana medicina* (Sevilla: Enrique Rasco, 1885), 51.

9. All translations are mine unless otherwise noted.

10. Jordi Salas-Salvado, "Diet and Dietetics in al-Andalus," *British Journal of Nutrition* 96, suppl. 1 (2006): s101.

11. Gerrit Bos, trans., *Maimonides on the Regimen of Health* (Leiden: Brill, 2019), 3.

12. Ibn Razīn al-Tugībī, *Relieves de las mesas, acerca de las delicias de la comida y los diferentes platos*, ed. and trans. Manuela Marín (Gijón: Ediciones Trea, 2007), 23.

13. Joan Santanach, ed., *The Book of Sent Soví: Medieval Recipes from Catalonia,* trans. Robin Vogelzang (Barcelona: Barcino-Tamesis, 2014), 15.

14. Carolyn Nadeau, *Food Matters: Alonso Quijano's Diet and the Discourse of Early Modern Spain.* (Toronto: University of Toronto Press, 2016), 23.

15. Alicia Martínez Crespo, ed., *Manual de mugeres en el qual se contienen muchas y diversas reçeutas muy buenas* (Salamanca: Universidad de Salamanca, 1995), 11.

16. Martínez Crespo, *Manual de mugeres*, 12.

17. Nadeau, *Food Matters*, 19.

18. David M. Gitlitz and Linda Kay Davidson, *A Drizzle of Honey: The Lives and Recipes of Spain's Secret Jews* (New York: St. Martin's Press, 1999), 11.

19. Eduardo Cerrato Casado, "El Calendario de Córdoba como fuente para la reconstrucción de la topografía eclesiástica de la Córdoba," in *Nasara, extranjeros en su tierra: Estudios sobre cultura mozárabe y catálogo de exposición* (Córdoba: Cabildo Catedral de Córdoba, 2018), 48.

20. Judah al-Harizi, *The Book of Tahkemoni: Jewish Tales from Medieval Spain,* trans. and ed. David Simha Segal (Portland: The Littman Library of Jewish Civilization, 2003), 551.

21. Al-Tugībī, *Relieves de las mesas*, 49.

22. Thomas Glick, *Islamic and Christian Spain in the Early Middle Ages* (Leiden: Brill, 2005), 103.

23. Olivia Remie Constable, "Food and Meaning: Christian Understandings of Muslim Food and Food Ways in Spain, 1250–1550," *Viator* 44, no. 3 (2013): 211.

24. Alfonso X, in his law code *Las Siete Partidas*, writes: "Et este pan a que llaman hostia ha de ser de farina de trigo" (And this bread that we call the Host must be made of wheat bread) (1:179–80).

25. Richard Terry Mount, "Levels of Meaning: Grains, Bread, and Bread Making as Informative Images in Berceo," *Hispania* 76, no. 1 (1993): 50–52.

26. Remie Constable, "Food and Meaning," 214.

27. Antonio Gázquez Ortiz, *La cocina en tiempos del Arcipreste de Hita* (Madrid: Alianza Editorial, 2002), 101.

28. Gitlitz and Davidson, *A Drizzle of Honey*, 29.

29. Quoted in Paul Freedman, *Out of the East* (New Haven: Yale University Press: 2008), 43.

30. Glick, *Islamic and Christian Spain*, 94.

31. Glick, *Islamic and Christian Spain*, 95.

32. Expiración García Sánchez, "El sabor de lo dulce en la gastronomía andalusí," in *La herencia árabe en la agricultura y el bienestar de Occidente* (Valencia: Universidad Politécnica de Valencia, 2002), 196.

33. Glick, *Islamic and Christian Spain*, 94.

34. Susan Rose, *The Wine Trade in Medieval Europe 1000–1500* (London: Continuum International, 2011), 154.

35. Brian Catlos, *Muslims of Medieval Latin Christendom, c. 1050–1614* (Cambridge: Cambridge University Press, 2014), 420.

Chapter 1

Meat and Mains

The more we enjoy the piglet
The better Catholics we become.[1]

The variety of meats that were available to a medieval household might be surprising to today's reader. Christians, Muslims, and Jews would be given the choice among multiple quadrupeds, like cows, goats, and sheep. Only Christians would be inclined toward pork, however. Among fowl, there were options for hens, chickens, partridges, doves, geese, and other small birds that were hunted or snared. Fish made up a large portion of the medieval diet, not only for its prevalence among rivers, streams, and lakes, but also because of its role in the Christian fast days. Wide varieties of water creatures were consumed, depending on geographical location and time of year.[2] Both Muslims and Christians would consume shellfish like shrimp, prawns, and snails. Eels, octopus, and tuna also made up a sizable percentage of medieval diets. Salted fish like cod, sardines, and anchovies provided sustenance especially during the long weeks of Lent. However, as Manuela Marín points out, seafood did not maintain the same social status that meat did at the tables of the wealthy.[3]

Although meat was seen as more of luxury, animal by-products were easily obtained. Dairy products were staples in the medieval diet (see figures 1.1 and 1.2). James Anderson writes that Spaniards ate a small breakfast that usually contained bread, sheep cheese, bacon (for Christians), and some wine. A rasher of bacon was served in every eating establishment and was inexpensive.[4]

The midday meal was around 1:00. The wealthy tended toward a heavier meal in the middle of the day because they did no hard labor after the meal. A variety of meats and other foodstuffs would mark the table as one of a prosperous family, as did a larder.[5]

Figure 1.1   A bucolic milking scene. The scene demonstrates the ubiquity of sheep rather than cows in the Middle Ages. *Source*: From the abridged Latinized MS Rome 4182 housed in the Biblioteca Casanatense in Rome.

For a comprehensive catalog of proteins available in the Middle Ages, we can turn to the fourteenth-century text *Libro de buen amor* or *The Book of Good Love*. In the middle of the text there is a parodic epic battle between doña Cuaresma (Lady Lent) and don Carnal (Lord Carnal). The troops involved in the battle are made up of commonly consumed foodstuffs in the Middle Ages.

The battle begins with a taunting letter by Lady Lent to meet Lord Carnal on the battlefield. Lord Carnal and his meaty troops must enter into battle with Lady Lent and her fishy and vegetable troops. Of course, Lady Lent is victorious, and the dread felt by many Christians faced with forty days of a restricted diet is represented by Carnal's loss of morale.

Lord Carnal counts among his troops a variety of meats:

Pusso en la delanteras muchos buenos peones,
gallynas e perdises, conejos e capones,
anades e lauancos, e gordos anssarones;
fasian su alarde cerca de los tysones.

En pos los escudados estan lo ballesteros,
las anssares, çeçinas, costados de carneros,

Figure 1.2   The cheese-making process. *Source*: From the abridged Latinized MS Rome 4182 housed in the Biblioteca Casanatense in Rome.

piernas de puerco fresco, los jamones enteros;
luego en pos de aqestos estan los caualleros.

las puestas de la vaca, lechones E cabritos
ally andan santando e dando grandes gritos;
luego los escudeiros, muchos quesuelos friscos,
que dan de las espuelas a los vinos byen tyntos.

Traya buena mesnada Rica de jnfançones,
muchos buenos faysanes, los locanos pauones;
venian muy byen guarnidos, enfiestos los pendones,
trayan armas estrañas e fuertes guarniçiones.[6]

Many foot soldiers filled the front rank,
hens and partridges, rabbits, and capons,
ducks both domestic and wild, fat geese too.
All formed their battle ranks near the burning embers.

Behind the shield-bearers came the archers,
dried, smoked goose, sides of mutton,

fresh legs of pork, whole hams.
Then after these came the knights;

Beefsteaks and chops of sucking pig and kid
all jostling and jumping, creating a fuss.
Then came the squires, the fresh black puddings,
spurring on the good red wines.

A splendid group of noblemen came after,
fine pheasants, lusty peacocks;
they were well-protected with their tail feathers spread,
and carried lofty weapons and strong armour.[7]

Unfortunately for Carnal's troops, the loss is a foregone conclusion, and they are humiliated and sent into hiding until the celebration of Easter.

Lady Lent has on her side a wide variety of sea creatures. Fish come from all over Iberia to aid Lent's cause. Through the detailing of Lent's troops, the reader is given an excellent geographic map of seafood varieties. For example, from Santander came the "vermilion lobsters," from Sevilla and Alcántara came bleaks and lampreys, and from Valencia came eels. Oysters, octopus, salmon, and even a whale come to the aid of Lent to finish off the morally ambiguous troops of Lord Carnal.

Fish was a mainstay of the medieval diet, and not just during Lent. According to market manuals in Toledo, fish made up 16.7 percent of food consumption in the fifteenth century.[8] Fishing was generally a male dominated activity, although the sale of fish was in the hands of women. Fish from the river was sold by weight and was very affordable. Preserved fish (*pescado cecial*) was in high demand, especially during Lent and other days of abstention. During these times, the prices of preserved fish were higher than fresh fish, whose prices also rose exponentially during those times.[9]

The variety available for consumption depended greatly upon the proximity to water. In the markets of Madrid, for example, river fish were easily found, but ocean fish was more likely dried or salted to prevent spoilage. Puñal Fernández tells us that until the late fifteenth century, few regulations were enforced on the selling of fish. Many people simply fished in the rivers and sold their fish from their homes (see figures 1.3 and 1.4). However, with the effort to modernize the urban center and regulate food sales in the late fifteenth century, more centralized fish markets (*pescaderías*) were created to control the quality and sale of fish.[10]

Another activity by which both rural and urban people supplemented their food supplies was hunting (see figures 1.5 and 1.6). Public access lands, although limited, were prime hunting grounds for the poor and middle class.

Figure 1.3 Fishing for lamprey. Illustration from an edition of *Theatrum Sanitatis* (fifteenth century). *Source*: From the abridged Latinized MS Rome 4182 housed in the Biblioteca Casanatense in Rome.

The nobility had their own lands on which to hunt and were often invited to hunt with royalty (see figure 1.7). However, laws were created to keep people off royal hunting grounds and those even suspected of hunting on these protected grounds were fined heavily.[11] Even so, butchers routinely sold venison, and game meats were commonly consumed in the urban center, which would demonstrate the inability to police all royal hunting grounds (think Robin Hood). Hunters used falcons, hawks, ferrets, dogs, and a variety of arms including crossbows, bows and arrows, blowguns, and traps.[12]

Hunting was divided into large game (*caza mayor*) and small game (*caza menor*).[13] Large game was allowed to royals and nobles only, and this category included anything larger than a fox, including deer and boar. Small game, like rabbits and birds, was allowed to commoners. Game animals make up some of Lord Carnal's troops:

vinieron muchos gamos e el fuerte jauali:
'Señor,' diz, 'non me escusedes de aquesta lyd a mi,

Figure 1.4 Fishing with nets. *Source*: From the abridged Latinized MS Rome 4182 housed in the Biblioteca Casanatense in Rome.

Figure 1.5 Hunting scene. *Source*: Fresco from Spain, twelfth century.

Figure 1.6   On hunting with dogs and snares. *Source*: *Livre de chasse* by Gaston Phébus.

que ya muchas vegadas lydie con don aly,
vsado so de lyd, syenpre por ende valy.'[14]

There were buck deer and wild boars:
"Sir, pray do not leave me out of the battle,
for I have fought many times with Mr. Moor,
I am used to battle and have fought well in the past."[15]

Those who lived in the mountains were allowed to hunt small game for themselves, but not to sell. Those who had a system of traps could sell their captured meat, but only on the dates between the festival of *San Miguel* (around the end of September) to *Carnestolendas* (Shrovetide—three days preceding Lent).[16] According to Izquierdo Benito, 12.4 percent of meat consumption in fifteenth-century Toledo came from hunting. Hunting was prohibited during the summer and Lent, however, and many were fined for off-season hunting.[17]

Judaism and Islam prohibited the consumption of blood, thus demanding a particular way of killing animals that allowed for the complete draining of

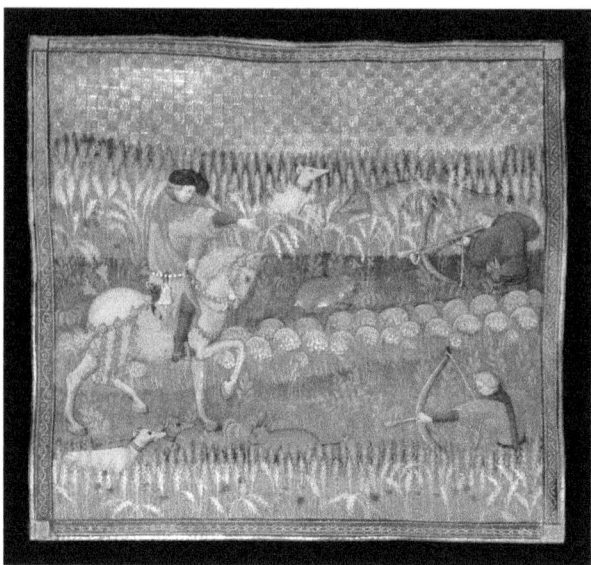

Figure 1.7   On hunting with bow and arrow. *Source*: *Livre de chasse* by Gaston Phébus.

blood from the animal. Gitlitz and Davidson tell us that in order for meat to
be kosher, it had to be drained of all blood and was often soaked in salted
water and drained in a wicker basket. Excess fat and the sciatic vein also had
to be removed.[18]

Muslim and Jewish health manuals made particular recommendations for
the consumption of meat. Ibn al-Khatíb's fourteenth-century text on health
and hygiene, *Libro de cuidado de la salud durante las estaciones* or *Libro
de higiene*, discusses the kinds of meats that should be consumed during
the year. In spring, for example, light meats like chicken, veal, and lamb
should be eaten.[19] In fall, chicken soup and other warming broths are recommended.[20] In winter, as one can imagine, soups should be replaced with fried
and roasted meats, and quadrupeds should be eaten.[21]

Olivia Remie Constable writes that before the conquest of Granada and
forced conversion, Muslims and Jews were allowed their own butchers and
separate communal ovens "lest forbidden items, especially items contain-
ing pork products, were cooked with licit foods."[22] After the conquest of
Granada, Muslim converts to Christianity, *moriscos*, were allowed their own
butchers, but, according to Harvey, those butchers were made to slaughter in
the Christian fashion. Later ordinances, however, would prohibit *moriscos*
from having separate butchers.[23]

In the *Siete Partidas*, Alfonso X's law code written in the thirteenth century, the king admonished Christians not to buy from non-Christian butchers.
There were a number of laws that regulated the religion of both the seller and

the buyer of meat in the thirteenth century. Many *fueros*, which were local laws and ordinances, prohibited Christian butchers from selling Jewish meat; prohibited Christian butchers from butchering meats for Jews during Carnival and Lent; and one, from Madrid, prohibited Christian butchers from selling meat rejected by Jewish butchers.[24] Further rules were put into place prohibiting Jews from buying fish on Fridays.[25]

By the late Middle Ages, slaughterhouses became more plentiful in the city. Butchering one's own meat became less tolerated and indeed outlawed by the end of the fifteenth century. Cleanliness and the method of slaughter became important issues. As medieval Iberia became more urbanized, the food supply became more regulated. In late medieval Madrid, slaughterhouses were located in a specific zone of the city, they had to have stone walls, and, according to Puñal Fernández, chalk was used to disinfect the floors.[26] There were also strict methods of killing and flaying the animal. Cows, for example, had to have their throats cut and be drained of blood before butchering. If this was done incorrectly, huge fines would be imposed.[27] With the introduction of the Inquisition, Jewish and Muslim converts were forced to buy meat from "old Christian" butchers (i.e., butchers of long Christian lineage), with a cleric standing by to ensure that the meat was butchered properly.[28]

Although, as Manuela Marín indicated, only the wealthy were able to consume large quantities of meat, the variety of meats available is truly surprising. In the following section, specific meats, fish, and meat by-products will be examined as they appear in medieval food manuals, scientific treatises, and popular literature.

PORK

For most Christian households, both rural and urban, owning a pig was feasible since pigs were the easiest and the most economical animal to raise. Puñal Fernández writes that pigs could forage for themselves, eating scraps, or could be fed simply on acorns or wild berries. The two most prized kinds of ham were the *ibérico* and the *céltico*. *Ibérico* was considered the most flavorful because of its "semi" wild nature, and it is still the most highly praised pork in today's markets.[29]

Pork was fraught with religious and social significance in the Middle Ages. Although a common enough meat, because of its religious prohibition among the Jews and the Muslims, pork became a sign at once of a Christian household and a well-managed household. According to Claudine Fabre-Vassas, "The pig incarnates a way of life; it is as much a sign of good domestic management and of Christian belonging; one never goes without the other."[30] In Juan de Aviñón's fifteenth-century medical treatise, *Sevillana medicina*, pork is cold and wet, which means that the meat is improved if the pig has maintained a steady diet of "drier" elements, such as acorns. In today's market, pigs that have foraged solely on acorns are highly prized (see figure 1.8). This observation demonstrates the intersection of medical knowledge and gastronomic tastes in medieval health manuals. Juan de Aviñon continues his chapter on pork by detailing the cuts of meats that are the healthiest, including the ears, the snout, the loin, and the ribs. Sausages, including blood sausage, were not as healthy unless they were seasoned with a variety of spices. Cured meats were fine, because of their warm and dry aspects.[31]

As a forbidden meat, one would think that pork would not make an appearance in Jewish or Muslim health manuals. Surprisingly, Maimonides praises pork as a superior meat for its humoral qualities. His advice, as we will see throughout this book, often puts physical attributes above religious constraints. He writes, "The best meat of land animals is pork; then comes the meat of kids and then that of calves. The meat of lambs is moist, sticky, and slimy. As for the meat of the other land animals, I recommend that anyone who cares about keeping his humors in a healthy condition avoid eating it."[32]

Christian food manuals provide a number of recipes that involve pork and pork by-products, which sets them apart from their Muslim counterparts of the same time period. Although Christian manuals demonstrate a strong

Figure 1.8   A man knocking acorns out of an oak tree to feed his pigs. From the *Psalter of Eleanor of Aquitaine* (c. 1185). *Source*: National Library of the Netherlands.

influence of Muslim cuisine, especially in the use of spices, recipes that contain pork and lard mark the texts as Christian (see figure 1.9).[33]

In Nola's fifteenth-century text, *Libro de cozina*, the first chapter discusses the ways in which servants should cut meat; and the first meat mentioned is bacon, followed by suckling pig. Throughout the book there are a variety of recipes for *potages* or stews, vegetable dishes, fish dishes, and stewed fruits. Many of the recipes, aside from those designated "for Lent," call for bacon as a common ingredient to flavor a number of dishes: from sautéed spinach to mutton casserole. It is interesting to note that many recipes that could be considered Muslim or Jewish dishes, have bacon as an ingredient to ensure their adherence to the Christian diet. One recipe *"Berengenas a la morisca"* (Eggplant in the Morisco style) suggests that the eggplant be sauteed with bacon. However, the recipe does note that olive oil can be used *"porque los moros no comen tocino"* (because the "Moors" don't eat bacon).[34]

A number of pork varieties can be counted among Lord Carnal's troops. In the aforementioned stanza 1084, the archers and the knights were legs of pork, whole hams, and suckling pigs. One of Lord Carnal's front lieutenants

Figure 1.9 The illumination shows a calendar for December and a man slaughtering a pig and singeing off his bristles. From the *Psalter of Eleanor of Aquitaine* (c. 1185). *Source*: National Library of the Netherlands.

is Lord Bacon, who brings with him troops entirely made up of pork products like smoked meats, pork chops, and pork loin:

Estaua don toçino con much otra çeçina,
çidierbedas e lomos, fynchida la cosina,
todos aperçebidos para la lyd malyna;
la dueña fue maestra, non vino tan ayna.[35]

Mr. Bacon was there with many other smoked meats,
pork chops and loin; the cooking pot was full,
all in readiness for the battle against the Marines.
The lady was skillful—she came later.[36]

References to pork appear often in satirical poetry of the fifteenth century to call out Judaizers and false converts. David Nirenberg writes that accusing someone of Judaizing or being a Jew was just one typical insult in a poetry of insults. Judaism, along with poetic incompetence, ignorance, rudeness, and sexual deviance were negative poles of poetic virtues.[37] An example of this kind of poetry can be found in the *Cancionero de Baena*. Juan Alonso de Baena, a convert and poet, writes these words about a convert he believes still practices his original faith: "*Presume muy ufano/palenciano,/cuando va por el camino./Come berças de tocino,/el mezquino,/por parescer a cristiano*" (This smug Palenciano boasts, when he travels, that he eats collards with bacon, that miserable man, to appear to be Christian.[38])

In the later fifteenth century, however, the poetry lost its playfulness and became a poetry of loathing. "Poetry ceased to be a place in which hermeneutic good faith could be proven."[39] Antón de Montoro's diatribe on the woes of being a convert written around 1474 reads:

Hice el credo y adorar, ollas de tocino grueso, torreznos a medio asar, oir misa y rezar, santiguar y persignar, y nunca pude matar este rastro de confeso.[40]

I communed and said the Creed. On fat bacon I did feed, half-cooked pork roast I did chew. I heard mass and prayed my beads crossed myself with industry, yet I never could succeed in shaking off the name of "Jew."

Montoro's efforts to demonstrate his Christian faith revolve around his need to ameliorate the sins of the tongue: he confesses, speaks the Creed, and he eats various types of pork. Regardless of these efforts, he is marked permanently as a Jew.

In the anti-*converso* screed titled *Libro llamado el Alborayque* written around 1488, the anonymous author condemns the new converts as neither Christian, nor Muslim, nor Jewish. He writes, "*Los conoceredes en sus fiestas, y en su guardar del sabado, y en su comer carne en quaresma, y en su meldar como judíos, y en los ayunos y pasquas guardar*" (You will know them because they keep the Sabbath and eat meat during Lent).[41] Not all converts are condemned, but rather, those who converted through force. These were the monsters who not only did not truly believe but also secretly worked against Christian conversion.

Alborayque comes from the name *Al-Burak*, the flying steed that carried Muhammed from Mecca to Jerusalem in one night. Gitlitz writes that by the fourteenth century, the beast "took on aspects of griffins, centaurs, or sphinxes."[42] Gitlitz compares the hybrid *Alborayque* to the perceived hybridism of the forced convert. The main attribute of the forced convert is hypocrisy. Gitlitz writes that Alborayque's first attribute, the wolf's mouth, indicates "*que son ypróquitas y falsos profetas, llamándose xrianos y no lo son; ca todo aquél ques uno y finge otro es ypócrita*" (that they are hypocrites and false prophets, calling themselves Christians even though they are not; because a person who is one thing and pretends to be another is a hypocrite).[43]

Another sign of the forced convert or *alborayque* is the kinds of foods it eats:

> *La XV señal del alborayque es que come de todos manjares. Assí los alboraycos comen Conejos, perdizes muertas de manos de xcristianos y de moros, y pescados—que ellos comen poco tocino—liebres y otros animals y aves, adafina como judíos; y cómenlo en todo tiempor: y enla quaresma delos cristianos y enel ayuno delos judíos y enel ayunto delos moros los más dellos, que pocos guardan las cerimonias delos otros.*[44]
>
> ----
>
> The fifteenth sign of the *Alborayque* is that they eat many kinds of foods. The *alborayques* eat rabbits, partridges killed by Christians and Muslims, and fish—they eat little bacon—hares, and other animals and birds, *adefina* like Jews, and eat it during all seasons: during the Christian Lent and during the fasts of the Jews and Muslims, and few maintain religious rituals of any kind.

The *alborayques* demonstrate their tenuous tie to Christianity through a diet that is defined more by Jewish tradition and ritual. References to pork products and their importance in the Christian diet may seem trivial to today's reader, but they go to the heart of the importance food and consumption played in the burgeoning notions of race and ethnicity in the Middle Ages.

FOWL

Medical treatises from all three religions agree that chicken soup is good for what ails you. The first line of Juan de Aviñon's chapter on fowl reads: "*Los gallos son provechosos para medicina*" (chickens are beneficial as medicine).[45] The text continues with the notions that the general temperament of fowl is warm and moist and that chickens should not be in cages as that will cause the meat to become melancholic and will engender a bad temper in the one who eats this bad meat.[46]

Both Christian and Muslim cookbooks contain a large number of recipes for poultry, and Gitlitz and Davidson write that they found references in Jewish documents to chicken, doves, geese, hens, and partridges.[47] Ibn Razīn's thirteenth-century *Relieves de las mesas, acerca de las delicias de la comida y los diferentes platos* contains seventy-nine recipes for fowl, including recipes for goose, hen, partridge, pigeon, ringdove, and thrush. In the *Book of Sent Soví*, the first recipe is for peacock sauce. The recipe is a complex mixture of chicken broth or broth made of mutton shanks with salt pork, thickened with almonds and spiced with a delicious array of fruit juices and spices. The first recipe is not only one that would probably have been served for special occasions but is also the most complex in the text.[48]

The ranks of birds in Lord Carnal's troops coincide with the class stratification of meats. The foot soldiers in Carnal's army were made up of the most common fowl, including geese, hens, capons, partridges, and ducks. These types of poultry were often raised domestically by small households and farms or snared in the wild.[49] The text indicates that both "domestic" and "wild" ducks participated.[50]

Pheasants and peacocks made up the "splendid group of noblemen" who took part in the battle.[51] These birds were more commonly found on noble and royal tables and were among the most celebrated dishes of the Middle Ages. In the *Cancionero de Baena*, these birds are mentioned as being common to hunt and pleasant to eat:

> *¿Cómo dexaré perdizes/en ivierno, que son sanas,/en verano codornices/de caçar por la mañanas/por ir con tales narices/a do biven las loçanas/que con sus grandes ufanas/a todo hombre dan su mate?*[52]
> ----
> How shall I ignore healthy winter partridges/in the summertime, quails,/hunting them in the morning/following one's nose to the wild ones' home/that with great vanity all men kill.

According to Juan de Aviñon, partridge is an excellent food given its warm and dry temperament. Interestingly, the quality of the partridge depends on how it was hunted. If hunted by a bird of prey or by crossbow, then the meat is much more desirable than if it was trapped, owing to the speed of its death.[53] This theory, which most likely came about through repeated observation, has actually been proven by modern science. Animals that die scared or trapped use up a higher level of glycogen, thus producing less lactic acid after death that tenderizes the meat.[54]

Aviñon lists a wide variety of fowl and their respective health benefits. *Pavón* (peacock) is tender and *"esfuerça el corazón"* (strengthens the heart); *Cordonizes y tórtolas* *"engendran buena sangre"* (quail and turtle doves produce healthy blood), and their meat is temperate. Aviñon writes that some people think quail meat is harmful because some Jews had died after eating the meat. Aviñon assures his readership that those Jews died not because of the quail, but because they had incurred the wrath of God.[55] Small birds, like sparrows, were plentiful, but Aviñon warns that their meat is neither satisfying nor terribly healthy.[56]

Maimonides has much to say about fowl and eggs. In his *Medical Aphorisms*, he makes the following observations:

> (68) "Boiled chicken soup balances the temperament."
> (69) "Sparrows are beneficial for paralysis," "and [also] increase sexual potency." "Soup [made] from larks loosens a colic. The nature of quails is close to that of sparrows; its [meat] is beneficial for healthy people and convalescents; its substance is fine; it dissolves kidney stones and stimulates micturition."
> (71) "The testicles of roosters provide extremely good nourishment and are the best food one can give to emaciated people and convalescents."[57]

The variety of fowl and their health benefits demonstrate the importance of birds both on the tables of nobility and humble folk.

It was uncommon to purchase chickens or hens since most households kept their own, especially to provide eggs since they were common in both sacred and secular meals. Eggs are commonly cited in connection with the Sabbath, funerals, Purim, and Passover. Gitlitz and Davidson write:

> *Huevos haminados* were a favorite dish of conversos of that time in Huete (Gudalajara) who prepared them by boiling eggs with onion skins, olive oil, and ashes, imparting a vermilion color and delicate onion flavor to the eggs. In Soria around the time of the expulsion, conversos prepared eggs similarly. This is still a favorite dish of Sephardic Jews of Turkey, who follow the same recipe.[58]

According to Aviñon, eggs are warm and humid and are good for the blood.[59] In the fifteenth-century *Manuel de mugeres*, copious numbers of eggs are called for to be used both in cooking and in balsams and unguents. Manuela Marín tells us that the use of eggs in *Relieves de las mesas* is one of its most striking characteristics and most likely a peculiarity of the *"gusto andalusí"* (palate of the Iberian Arabs) rather than a common element in Arab cooking of the time.[60]

Indeed, if we think of perhaps the most iconic dish of today's Spanish tapas bar, the famous egg and potato tortilla comes to mind instantly. Eggs are incorporated into every kind of dish. Although in *Relieves de las mesas*, only eleven recipes call for eggs as the main dish, the book contains a large number of recipes that include eggs, everything from stews and soups, to forming parts of stuffing for a variety of meats, to sweets and pastries. Some recipes call for up to thirty eggs for one dish. Marín cautions us to remember, however, that like the consumption of meat, this overabundance of egg use was found only in aristocratic diets.[61]

BEEF

Like lamb, beef was one of the staples of the Iberian diet. Gitlitz and Davidson tell us that more people in Iberia ate beef than in any other country in the area.[62] Cattle, like sheep, were raised both for their meat and for their milk. However, if we are to take the cooking manuals as a guide for the popularity of certain foodstuffs, we can see that, for example, the number of recipes using beef in the *Relieves de las mesas* is significantly smaller than the number of recipes for sheep, lamb, or goat (ten versus sixty-three).[63] There are no recipes in the *Sent Soví* that feature beef specifically. A general recipe for tripe calls for veal, mutton, or beef.[64] Meat flavorings in this collection tend toward chicken-based broths or pork grease. In the appendix that includes missing recipes from the *Sent Soví* tradition, a recipe for cabbage calls for beef grease.[65] Generally, though, beef is not a significant part of the *Sent Soví* collection.

A number of recipes in *A Drizzle of Honey* call for beef, although mostly in the form of stews. In some of these recipes, lamb can be used in place of beef. One recipe calls for the use of beef liver. Gitlitz and Davidson remind us that all "edible parts of animals were served throughout the Middle Ages and extant recipe books contain directions for how to serve tripe, livers, kidneys, lungs, spleen, and other innards."[66] In *Libro de buen amor*, beefsteaks are mentioned as part of Carnal's troops, acting as knights.[67]

The raising of beef became more popular after the Reconquest but started with the Romans. Moving cattle could be done easily and quickly, which made animal herding popular in times of uncertainty and war. Agriculture was practiced once land had been fully established under one ruler. From the twelfth century on, treatises among Christians and Muslims were created to allow for animal herding and movement through each other's lands.[68] Four specific routes for transhumance of both cattle and sheep were established along old Roman mountain passes. By the thirteenth century, the foundation of the powerful union of sheepherders, *La Mesta*, was established.[69] Beef and lamb were such an important part of the Iberian diet that to raise money for the Christian wars against the Muslims, the papacy temporarily granted contributors an exemption from rules prohibiting eating meat on Friday or during Lent.[70]

Beef in Aviñon's treatise is not as good for one's health as some other meats. Aviñon specifically states that most beef is eaten in Castile, which demonstrates the importance of cattle herding in the fifteenth century. Medically speaking, veal is better for one's health than cow, as the meat is warm and humid and *"conviértese en buen humor"* (has good humoral qualities).[71] Aviñon states that oxen, like veal, was easier on the system than cows, but in Castile, again, they were not eaten as often as cows. Rather, oxen were used more as beasts of burden. Bulls maintained a ritual importance in the Middle Ages and were used for entertainment and also for sacrificial slaughter. Although bullfighting as we know it today did not yet exist, events like running with bulls and entering into corrals with them to prove one's courage took place during feast days and celebrations. Bulls were also slaughtered on religious holidays and to celebrate political victories like the defeat of the Muslims in Granada.[72] According to literary texts of the fifteenth century, the meat of bulls was to be served only to the poor because of its toughness and its saltiness.[73]

SHEEP

Thomas Glick writes:

> Both Muslims and Christians practiced transhumant herding. Transhumance crossed the frontiers in the twelfth century with a shift in the balance in powers. Christians entered into al-Andalus with herds of sheep. The rise of transhumance in Christian kingdoms was a result of the process of land clearance and cultivation of cereal, vineyards and orchards. Lay and ecclesiastical lords fenced off their pastures. Monasteries owned large herds. By the eleventh century, the herd of San Millán was so large that it was able to supply the royal palace with 600 sheep, 100 hogs and 80 cows in 1049 without making a dent in the herd.[74]

Sheep proved to be the most profitable animal raised by Muslims, Jews, and Christians in the Middle Ages. Not only was the meat accepted by all three religions, but also its by-products of milk, cheese, and wool allowed for great profit. Iberia provided wool for the "insatiable textile factories" of Italy and the Netherlands.[75] Merino wool was introduced to Europe by the Berbers of North Africa.[76]

Arab cooking manuals privilege mutton and lamb over beef. Christian food manuals, like the *Book of Sent Soví* contain a variety of recipes for mutton stew, kid meat pluck (organ meat), and fritters of goat. Some recipes also call for salted pork to be added to the stew, which would mark the recipe as

Christian. Meatballs or *albóndigas* were made with both beef and lamb. *El carnero* or mutton was, according to Puñal Fernández, "*el rey de las carnes,*" the king of meats.[77] Aviñon writes, "*El carnero es más noble de las carnes de las animalias que andan en cuatro piés*" (Mutton is the noblest of all the meats that come from animals that walk on all fours). The meat is temperate and "*esfuerça la calentura natural del coraçon*" (strengthens the natural warmth of the heart).[78]

In the later Middle Ages, there were strict rules about when a sheep could be slaughtered. Under a year was considered too young, but a *borrego*—a yearling—was allowed, especially during times of shortage.[79] The beauty of the sheep was that the medieval household could use every part of it: its wool was sought after at home and abroad; its skin was used for leather and parchment; and its milk was created into the most delicious cheese. Market manuals of the fifteenth century note that the male goat was more sought after than the female, but lamb was the most appreciated. Puñal Fernández lists the prices of mutton higher than beef, but lamb was priced higher than goat or mutton.[80]

There are two sections in *Libro de buen amor* that specifically mention sheep and lamb in the context of food. Carnal escapes his imprisonment and hides for a while in the Jewish quarter during Lent. The Rabbi lends him a horse to escape, and he rides through Extremadura, well known for its sheepherding:

pusose muy priuado en extremo de medellyn;
dijeron los corderos: 'vedes aqui la fyn.'

Cabrones e cabritos, carneros e ovejas
dauan grandes balidos, desien estas conssejas:
'sy nos lyevuas de aqui, Carnal, por las callejas,
a muchos de nos otros tirara las pellejas.'[81]

He rode like a flash to the depths of Medellín.
All the lambs bleated: "Baa! This is the end of me!"

Billy-goats and kids, rams and ewes
all bleated loudly and spoke as follows:
"If Carnal takes us from here through the streets,
many of us will lose our skins."[82]

Carnal's return is celebrated at the end of Lent. He is met with great joy by all the butchers, tripe-sellers, shepherds, and other meat purveyors. Carnal does not disappoint:

Enderedor traya, çeñida de la su çynta,
vna blanca rrodilla, esta de sangre tynta;

al cablon que esta gordo el muy gelo pynta,
fase fase: ¡ve! bailando en bos E doble quinta.[83]

Girdled round his waist he wore
a white cloth stained with blood,
bringing fearful forebodings to the plumpest goat,
who bleats and baas in melody and counterpoint.[84]

The medieval meat market is depicted in delicious detail in gate 21 of Judah al-Harizi's *Book of Tahkemoni*. In this story, al-Harizi's itinerant protagonist fools a passing peasant into paying for his lamb dinner. Hever the Kenite invites the Arab peasant to the meat market to share a delicious repast. Al-Harizi describes the moment in which the two men find the roasting lamb ready to eat:

> Momentarily, amidst the market's crush and jam we found, dripping on a spit, a gorgeous lamb. The fire's tongue set its innards steaming and our tongues dreaming: with its hot powers it raised up meaty flowers displaying morsels thick and choice, tender and moist, snow-white within, ruby-red outside, ruby and diamond riches side by side, the fatty cover gleaming white, a rare delight, an awesome, holy sight designed to split the heart apart.[85]

We can almost taste the meat dripping its fat into the fire. Hever and the peasant glut themselves with lamb, bread, and dates for dessert, but the poor peasant is stuck with the bill.

Ibn Quzmān, one of the most famous andalusí poets, wrote *zéjeles*, or strophic poems that narrated the poet's day-to-day existence. María Jesús Rubiera Mata writes that Quzmān's poetry is one of the best sources we have of the documentation of typical foods consumed during the twelfth century.[86] In Arabic texts, like Ibn Quzmān's poetry, meat is not mentioned as often as bread and legumes. María Jesús Rubiera Mata believes that this could be because meat was seen as a luxury product, out of reach financially for most poets. The meat Ibn Quzmān does mention most often, however, is mutton (*carnero*). Rubiera Mata writes that the Muslims used mutton the way Christians used pork: every part was used, including the rendering of the fat and preserving the meat with salt.[87] Ibn Quzmān's *zéjel* 8 reads:

¡Oh aquél a quien ver me da alegría!
Preciso mi carnero para degollar.

Preciso me es la asadura arrancar,
comer asado de bofes,
hacer caldo de la cabecilla
y colgar cecina en mi azotea.[88]

Oh you, what happiness when I see you!
I must have a sheep to sacrifice.

It is necessary to cut some to roast,
to taste some of its roasted innards,
and to make a soup of its little head,
and to hang strips of meat from the rafters.

The sheep is the perfect animal to prepare for the great festival of *Eid al Adha*. The poet tells us of the different delicacies that can be made from the sheep for this special occasion including the innards and curing the extra meat.

   Although mutton and lamb were staples of the medieval diet, by the fifteenth century, these meats became markers of Jewish and Muslim diets. Remie Constable uses a list of foods found in the sixteenth-century work *La Lozana Andaluza* as an example of Muslim and Jewish foods that maintained their presence in the Iberian diet. The main character, Aldonza, reminisces about her childhood kitchen in Granada. In Aldonza's nostalgic list of foods there are a number of dishes made with mutton and lamb. She mentions breast of mutton, stuffed goat tripe, giblets, and young roasted goat flavored with Ceuta lemons. This list, according to Remie Constable, is typical of Muslim diets of late medieval Iberia.[89] These dishes would also have been common at Jewish tables, although the offal would need to be free of any blood.

FISH

The medieval Christian calendar could be divided between meat days and fish days. Holy days, feast days, and Lent called for a vegetarian or pescatarian diet. Muslims were unlikely to enjoy fish as much as Christians. García Sánchez writes that in the *Tratado de la cocina hispano-magrebi*, out of five hundred recipes, only about twenty deal with fish in any capacity. She does note, however, that fish did make up a larger percentage of the diets of Muslims who lived on the coast.[90] The options for Jewish cooks were more limited in the area of seafood:

> Jewish and crypto-Jewish cooks in Iberia were constrained in their choices by the rules of kashrut, according to which the permissible fish must have both gills and scales. This eliminates perhaps half of the seafood routinely consumed by Christian Iberians: octopus and squid, eels, rays, skate, shark and catfish, all mollusks and crustaceans.[91]

In medical treatises, fish was not as highly sought out as meat. According to humoral theory, fish was, as one can imagine, cold and wet. In order to mollify one's fiery temper, a cold and wet foodstuff might be prescribed. On the whole, however, these kinds of foods were to be eaten in smaller portions. Juan Cruz Cruz writes that fish were divided into two sections: salt- and freshwater, and saltwater fish were more highly prized, not only for flavor, but for its humoral quality that was drier, given that they were fished from salty seas.[92]

According to Juan de Aviñon, fish maintain a varying degree of qualities depending on the kind of water they are fished from and the quality itself of the flesh. In his chapter on fish, he mentions ten kinds of freshwater fish and twenty-seven kinds of saltwater fish and shellfish. Each one is described by its humoral nature, the kind of person who should eat the fish, and how it should be prepared for maximum health benefits. Freshwater fish are better for the old and infirm and for those who were fierier of temper. For those who needed more fire in their blood, saltwater fish were best.[93] Maimonides claims that rockfish, because of its high digestibility, "is extremely good and beneficial in preserving the health of a human body since it produces blood of an intermediate consistency, neither thin and fine nor thick."[94]

Medical advice often intersected with cooking preferences. In the *Sevillana medicina*, not only does Aviñon provide an exhaustive list of fresh- and saltwater fish, but he also includes the manner in which they should be eaten. Recipes that one would find in a cookbook are found in this medical treatise. For example, trout, the "mutton" of the fish world, according to Aviñon, could be fished year-round, had a temperate flesh and a good flavor. Sturgeon, according to Aviñon, is the "beef" of the fish world and is best cooked after marinating in white wine and oregano.[95]

In the saltwater category, tuna is not recommended as it is "melancholic" in nature and of little nutritional value. Salmon, however, is recommended for those who are ill, and its flesh is both warm and humid. Saltwater fish seem trickier, and Aviñon warns that certain fish are only appropriate for those who are consumptive (like bass) or those who suffer from loss of appetite (like sardines).[96]

In *Libro de buen amor*, the majority of Lent's troops are made up of fish, which shows the incredible variety that, in theory, was available to the medieval household. In the heat of the battle we are told that "*la salada sardina*" (the salted sardine) wounded "*la gruesa gallyna*" (the fat hen)[97]; "*de parte de valençia venien las anguillas*" (the Valencian eels) "*dauan a don carnal por medio de las costillas*" (attacked Carnal in the ribs)[98]; "*ay andaua el atun commo vn bravo leon/fallose con don tosino, dixole much baldon*" (the tuna went about like a ferocious lion/encountered Mr. Bacon gave him the same abuse)[99]; and "*ally lidian las ostyas con todos los conejos,/con la liebre justauan los asperos cangrejos*" (the oysters fought with the rabbits,/the hard-shelled crabs jousted with the hare).[100] When looking at the fish markets of the time, the most commonly sold fish was the salted sardine. According to Puñal Fernández, there was a massive consumption of cured/salted sardines among the lower classes. Other commonly purchased fish were a variety of eels, dogfish, and sea bream.[101]

Around Madrid there were many rivers from which folks could fish during certain times of the year and then sell from their own homes. It wasn't until the 1490s that regulations for the sale of fish were more controlled.[102] Dried fish, however, was always in high demand, as it did not spoil easily.[103] Salted fish was also one of the staples of the Lenten diet. When Lord Carnal reappears on Easter morning, the people celebrate with glee because his appearance signals the end of Lent and privation, which included, of course, a virtuous diet:

Venia don carnal en carro muy preciado,
cobierot de pellejos e de cueros çercado,
el buen enperador esta arremangado,
en saya, faldas en çinta, e sobra byen armado.

Tenia coffya en la cabeça, quel cabello nol ssaga,
queça tenie vestida blanca e Raby galga,
en el su carro otro a par del non caualga,
a la llybre que saleluego le echa la galga.[104]

Carnal traveled in a priceless chariot,
covered in skins and lapped in leather.
The good emperor had rolled up his sleeves.
He wore a tunic and belt and carried powerful weapons.

He had a butcher's hat on his head to keep his hair in,
and wore a white cloak, long as a greyhound's tail.
No equal rode with him on his chariot.
He set his greyhound at once on any hares that emerged.[105]

Lord Carnal is shunned by good Christians during Lent, yet his triumphant return at Easter proves that although gluttony was seen as disharmonious to the social order, ultimately his company, and all that it implies, was most certainly preferred to the company of Lady Lent.

RELIGIOUS IMPLICATIONS

The consumption of and abstention from meat in the Middle Ages can be seen as the cause of everything from crises of conscience to death. C. M. Woolgar writes:

> One of the earliest and continuing determinants of eating patterns was the link between diet and virtue. From at least the fourth century, Christianity promoted abstinence for its spiritual benefits. Refraining from meat and dairy fats, and hence from carnality and its associated vices of gluttony and lechery, helped to ensure the salvation of the soul.[106]

In any given year, there were over two hundred fast days in the Christian calendar. During these days, good Christians were expected to follow a vegetarian diet and to be sparing in drink and sexual intercourse.

The longest fast period was, of course, Lent. Bridget Ann Henisch writes that in the Middle Ages, Lent was considered "a long and dreary stretch of time, to be endured as a penance; a quite considerable sacrifice to be offered up to God in gratitude for His mercies, and sorrow for man's inadequacies."[107] It may be hard to imagine a time in which one could be punished for breaking the fast during Lent. During the Middle Ages, the Lenten season was often met with outward piety but inward dread. Along with eschewing foods that were seen to breed lust, overly warming in their effects, sexual pleasure was also curtailed. These forty days of fasting were an important *imitatio Christi* that all Christians were required to perform before the joyous feast of Easter. The privations of Lent, especially to those who could not obtain a variety of vegetarian foodstuffs or fresh fish, were harsh at best. And the punishments to those who dared to break the fast ranged from whippings to pulled teeth. Returning to the battle of Carnal and Lent, we can see that the subtext of the depictions of Carnal as a robust and sexual man and Lent as a pinched and chastising woman demonstrate the common notion that the Lenten season brought with it the rejection of all that is pleasurable.

Gluttony was often associated with meat eating in the Middle Ages (see figure 1.10). To be abstemious was to reject meat and other delicacies. Our poor Lord Carnal was accused of gluttony by Lady Lent. At the outset of the Lent/Carnal scenes, she sends him a letter of challenge that reads:

De mi doña quaresma, justiçia de la mar,
alguaçil de las almas que se han de saluar,
a ty, carnal goloso, que te non coydas fartar,
enbyo te el ayuno por mi des-afiar.[108]

From Lent, Justice of the Sea,
bailiff of souls which must be saved,
to you, *greedy Carnal,* never sated with eating,
I send Mr. Fasting to challenge you.[109]

Upon amassing his troops, Carnal sits down to a gluttonous feast before the battle.

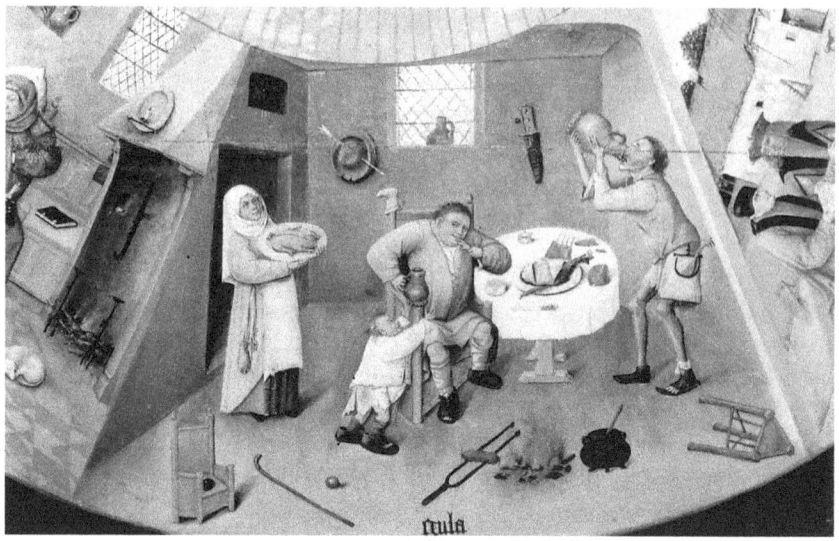

Figure 1.10   Gula (gluttony): Eating and drinking to excess. *Source*: Detail from the painting titled *The Seven Deadly Sins and the Four Last Things*, attributed to Hieronymus Bosch, c. 1500.

Estaua don carnal Rica mente assentado,
a messa mucho farta en vn Rico estrado,
delante sus juglares, commo omne onrrado;
desas muchas vyandas era byen abastado.[110]

Carnal was luxuriously seated.
His table was abundant, in an elegant room.
He had a good supply of all the meats
while minstrels played before him as before an honored man.[111]

Once Lent arrives, however, Carnal is hard-pressed to begin the battle, so indulgent was his feast:

Commo avia el buen omne Sobra mucho comido,
con la mucha vianda mucho vino ha veuido,
estaua apesgado e estaua adormido,
por todo el su Real entro el apellido.[112]

Since the good man had eaten too much,
and drunk a lot of wine with all the meat,
he felt very heavy and sleepy
as the war cry rang throughout his camp.[113]

The sin of gluttony, associated with Carnal and his immoderate diet, represented the sins of all who dared to overeat. Once Lent started, Carnal was forced to follow a penitential diet that would have resonated with the archpriest's contemporary audience: Lentils, chickpeas, greens, bread, and water.[114] The Catalan moralist Francesc Eiximenis gives an example of how to avoid gluttony: one must forsake banqueting and "costly meats, such as fowl, the very best fish, and sauces, and all expensive wines and exquisite breads."[115] Alfonso Martínez de Toledo also warns against loving meat too much.[116]

Fasting, then, became a time to control the excesses of one's particular temperament. This proved to be part of a healthy diet as well as religiously necessary. As Terence Scully writes, "The scientific argument that can be elaborated by the mid-thirteenth century in order to rationalize a long-established religious practice shows just how thoroughly a learned understanding of the physical nature of man could be incorporated into theological doctrine."[117]

St. Isidore of Seville wrote that eating meat bred the lust of the carnal. Red meat, by its very nature warm and moist, led to the overheating of a person, especially those whose temperaments were sanguine or choleric (like our poor Lord Carnal) and was thus associated with gluttony and lust. Medieval theologians were careful not to condemn meat outright, since it was a creation of God, but focused on its humoral quality in order to eschew it during fasts and Lent.

According to Caroline Walker Bynum, abstinence meant "dry-eating," that is, bread, salt, and water.[118] Extreme monastic fasting reflected this dry eating, but fasting practices became less stringent during the later Middle Ages. Nevertheless, meat, and its warming by-products like lard, milk, butter, eggs, and cheese were strictly forbidden during Lent and on Fridays throughout the year. "To violate the Friday fast," writes Walker Bynum, "was the clearest way of rejecting the faith."[119]

Foods that increased the negative elements of one's temperament were as "dangerous to one's moral health" as to one's physical health.[120] Regardless of religious conviction or medical advice, however, the people of the Middle Ages worked hard to augment the list of acceptable foods during Lent. As Henisch writes, "Belt tightening and salt herrings wreaked havoc on the human spirit."[121] If one lived far from a water source, fresh fish could be hard to afford. Medieval cooks were clever in their ability to substitute almond milk for animal milk and to create various "false" dishes like mock eggs made of boiled almond milk and bacon made from shredded fish. Definitions of fish too were expanded throughout the Middle Ages. Fish included whale, dolphin, beaver's tail, and barnacle goose.[122]

Not maintaining Lent or Christian feast days became one of the markers of so-called false converts in the fifteenth century. As life became more difficult for the Jews, conversion seemed a way out of their predicaments. Inquisition testimony states that one of the worst crimes of the convert is not keeping Lent or eating meat on Fridays or other fast days. Edicts of Faith published in the fifteenth century listed a wide array of Judaizing customs that included eating meat during Lent and refusing to eat pork.

The origins of the pork taboos in both Judaism and Islam are convoluted at best. There are both anthropological and religious explanations. Mary Douglas writes that taboos are created to establish "a separate, holy and supernatural world, which is given concrete expression in the taboo." The specificity of the taboo ensures an orderly, "holy" world.[123] The Mosaic taboo is often given an Egyptian origin. Among the Egyptian nobility, there may have already been a taboo, which Moses could have maintained after fleeing.[124] The formal pork taboo appears in the Torah or Old Testament in mid-fifth century BCE in *Leviticus* 11:

> And HaShem spoke unto Moses and Aaron, saying to them: Speak unto the children of Israel, saying: These are the living things which ye may eat among all the beasts that are on the earth. Whatsoever parteth the hoof, and is wholly cloven-footed, and cheweth the cud, among the beasts, that may ye eat. Nevertheless, these shall ye not eat of them that only chew the cud or of them that only part the hoof: the camel, because he cheweth the cud but parteth not the hoof, he is unclean unto you. And the rock badger . . . and the hare . . . and the swine, because he parteth the hoof and is cloven-footed but cheweth not the cud, he is unclean to you. Of their flesh ye shall not eat, and their carcasses ye shall not touch; they are unclean unto you.[125]

Pre-Islamic North Africans raised and ate pigs. However once Islam replaced local religions, the pork taboo became a part of the landscape, both literally and figuratively. Pigs were no longer raised by Muslims, but rather, by religious minorities. The Qur'an specifically states a prohibition of the flesh of swine in Sura 5: "Forbidden to you are carrion, blood, and swine; what is slaughtered in the name of any other than Allah; what is killed by strangling, beating, a fall, or by being gored to death; what is partly eaten by a predator unless you slaughter it; and what is sacrificed on altars."[126]

Freidenreich writes that the Qur'an "establishes proper food practices as a divinely ordained golden mean between two undesirable extremes, the former being false and the latter excessively rigorous (idolaters and Jews)."[127] In early Christianity, too, rejecting the Hebrew Bible's dietary laws furthered the "distinction between Christians and Jews."[128]

The eschewing of pork by Muslims and Jews was perhaps one of the most damning behaviors during the fifteenth century. Newly converted families hung hams in their doorways to prove that they had truly accepted the Christian faith.[129] But the pork question prejudiced Christians against the Jews especially and servants kept their eyes open for dishes served without pork or cooked in olive oil instead of lard.

The consumption of all foods is what defined Christians as "not-Jews" and affirms the authority of the New Testament statements about food, such as "For the pure all things are pure" (Tit. 1:15, Mark 7:19, 1 Tim. 4:4).[130] Food abstention or, indeed, substitution, at the end of the fifteenth century marked one as a Judaizer or false convert in the eyes of the Christian Church. According to Freidenreich, the use of impurity rhetoric in order to distinguish the other can be divided into three categories: intrinsic, circumstantial (polluted), and offensive (defiled).[131] Much can be learned from the ways in which these categories were employed to designate the other.

Early Christians marked themselves as different from Jews precisely for their acceptance of all foods. Both Muslims and Jews shared the taboo against pork, but Jewish dietary laws condemn many more foods as intrinsically impure. Medieval Christians were more likely to condemn foods for their circumstantial impurity, food that came in contact with something undesirable. Circumstantial pollution for medieval Jews had to do with unclean practices such as meat coming in contact with blood and unclean cooking and butchering processes. Similarly, medieval Muslims required their own butchering techniques but had fewer food restrictions. Muhammad Khalid Masud explains the terminology used in the Qur'an:

> The Qur'ån uses two terms: haram (forbidden) and khaba'ith (pl of kabith), unclean for the legal evaluation of prohibited food. Legal food: halal (lawful) and tayyib (pure). Two other terms: fisq (impiety) and rijs (dirty) are also used for the prohibited sacrificial meat and wine respectively.[132]

Offensive or defiled food comes from the likelihood that a particular food or drink was used in an idolatrous ceremony. Practitioners of all three religions were admonished to shun food associated with sacrifice and idol worship.[133]

In the twelfth century, the *converso* Petrus Alfonsi, in his *Dialogue against the Jews,* uses his knowledge of Christian, Muslim, and Jewish religious texts to argue against the pork taboo. Alfonsi claims that with the advent of Christ "all meats ought to be permitted and eaten."[134] The Twelfth *Titulus* of the *Dialogue* states, "As Christ came, however, and cleansed the bodies of believers by baptism and infused the fullness of the Holy Spirit, now the person's body cannot be defiled or dulled by any meat."[135] The convert's argument, predicated on the perceived inherent righteousness of Christianity, seemingly puts an end to further discussion about food taboos from the Christian perspective.

After the arrival of the Inquisition to Iberia in 1478, the consumption of certain foodstuffs became life threatening. Andrés Bernáldez, a priest of

Seville and the author of *Historia de los Reyes Católicos*, used food customs as one justification for the expulsion of 1492:

> *ansí eran tragones y comilones, que nunca perdieron el comer á costumbre judáica de manjarejos é olletas de afinas, manjarejos de cebollas é ajos, é fritos con aceite, y la carne guisaban, con aceite, é lo echaban en lugar de tocino é de grosura por escusar el tocino; y el aceite con la carne es cosa que hace muy mal oler el resuello; y ansí sus casa y puertas hedian muy mal á aquellos man-jarejos; y ellos ese mesmo tenian el olor de los judios por causa de los manjares y de no ser baptizados.*[136]
>
> ----
>
> In this manner, they were gluttons and great drinkers, who never lost the Judaic custom of eating victuals, with earthen jars of stewed meats, onion and garlic dishes, fried in oil. And the meat they would cook in oil, and they would substitute it in place of bacon and tallow so as to avoid eating pork. The meat with oil is a thing that causes a very bad odor to one's breathing. Thus, their houses and doors stunk very badly with these dishes. They themselves had the odor of the Jews because of the dishes and because of not being baptized.[137]

In 1492, Jews were given four months to get their affairs in order and leave the country. The Edict of Expulsion makes no mention of conversion as a means of staying in the country, but many Jews did indeed convert to Christianity. Luis Suárez Fernández writes that the Jews had "four months to make the most terrible decision of their lives: to abandon their faith to be integrated in it [in the kingdom, in the political and civil community], or leave the territory in order to preserve it."[138]

Muslims did not have to make this choice until a decade later. Forced conversion created a population of crypto-Jews and crypto-Muslims. James Amelang writes that the "destruction of Islamic customs was essential" to the well-being of the Christian minority in Granada. Therefore, as early as 1508, laws were enacted that decreed the destruction of the Arabic language as well as the prohibition of dietary prescriptions, including ritual slaughter.[139]

Both Muslim and Jewish women become targets of the Inquisition soon after its arrival in Iberia. Because they were in charge of shopping and cooking, and maintaining the household and the kitchen, women were easier targets for spies, especially among their own servants. Food prohibitions and rituals surrounding food preparation were some of the most ingrained habits among Muslims and Jews. Mary Elizabeth Perry writes that children of *morisco* families "had learned an embodied self-knowledge from certain Islamic rituals and Muslim cultural practices that would be considered apostasy."[140] "Both boys and girls," writes Perry, "learned Muslim taboos against consuming pork and, in some regions, wine . . . but really it was the girls who learned how to prepare foods in oil rather than in fat."[141] Amelang writes that *morisca* women were known as *dogmatizadoras*, or keepers of religious tradition.[142] It is clear that they also were the keepers of culinary traditions that became ingrained in daily life.

The primary reason for the arrival of the Inquisition to Iberia was to root out false converts, especially among the Jews, and, ostensibly, to prevent "reversion" to old ways or contagion of Christians. Madera Allan writes that even years before the Tribunal was founded, keeping kosher was controversial.[143] The "litmus test for religious loyalty," continues Allen, was "dietary defilement."[144] Food and food practices became, then, one of the most common ways to distinguish between Us and Them. And to be one of "them" was to face punishment, and even, death. Inquisition trial testimonies are filled with accusations of Judaizing activities that involved food, including cooking on Fridays, cleaning and preparing meat by cutting away fat or veins, not eating strangled birds, and, of course, not eating pork.

Spanish proverbs abound with references to Jews and their relationship to pork:

> *Puerco en casa judía, hipocresía.*/Pork in a Jewish household is hypocrisy.
> *Con misa ni tocino no convides al judío.*/Neither for mass nor for bacon do you invite a Jew.
> *No temblés tocino, decía el judío, que no hay en casa quien mal os haga.*/Don't tremble bacon, said the Jew, because no one will do you harm in this house.[145]

The anti-Semitic invective of the fifteenth century demonstrates the strong ties between food and identity. In the *Coplas de Román contra el Ropero*, Román accuses the Ropero of being a Judaizer:

Trobar redonda mesilla,
trobar olla que no quiebre,
trobar nunca con anguilla
ni mucho menos con liebre.
Trobar en ser carnicero
como la ley ordeno,
trobar an comer carnero
degollado caraldio
qual vuestro padre comio.[146]

Sing of a round table,
sing of a pot in which one will not find eel nor hare.
Sing of a butcher
who follows the ritual laws,
sing of eating mutton
that has been butchered correctly
like your father used to eat.

In this one poem, the poet gives us multiple clues to the behavior of the perceived false convert: he won't eat eel or hare, and buys meat only from an approved butcher, one who prepares the meat by draining the blood from the neck, from a butcher who would have sold meat to his father. Other examples of rhetoric mention the maintenance of religious rituals. Again, Bernáldez uses food customs to justify Christian outrage:

Hedían como judíos; no comian puerco si no fuese en lugar forzoso; comian carne en las cuaresmas y vigilias é cuatro témporas de secreto; guardaban las pascuas y sábados como mejor podian; enviaban aceite á las sinagogas para las lámparas; . . . tenian judíos rabies que les degollaban las reses é aves para sus negocios; comian pan cençeño al tiempo de los judios, carnes tajeles; hacian todas las ceremonias judíaicas, de secreto en cuanto podían.[147]

They would not eat pork unless forced to do so; they ate meat during Lent, vigils, and the Catholic seasonal fast days. They observed the Passover and Sabbaths as best they could. They sent oil to the synagogues for the lamps. . . . They had Jewish rabbis who would ritually slaughter their cattle and fowl for their affairs. They ate unleavened bread at the appointed Jewish times, and specially prepared meats.[148]

The consumption of meat served as a flashpoint in the religious strife of the late Middle Ages. Jews and Muslims were accused simultaneously of being too abstemious and being gluttonous. Remie Constable writes that Muslims were considered both luxurious and uncivilized, attractive and repulsive.[149] In the fifteenth century, the conflation of consumption habits with religion justified the movement toward wiping out all religions other than Christianity.

NOTES

1. From an eighteenth-century Burgundian song. Quoted in Claudine Fabre-Vassas, *The Singular Beast*, trans. Carol Volk (New York: Columbia University Press, 1997), 247.

2. David M. Gitlitz and Linda Kay Davidson, *A Drizzle of Honey: The Lives and Recipes of Spain's Secret Jews* (New York: St. Martin's Press, 1999), 83.

3. Ibn Razīn al-Tugībī, *Relieves de las mesas, acerca de las delicias de la comida y los diferentes platos*, ed. and trans. Manuela Marín (Gijón: Ediciones Trea, S.L.: 2007), 43.

4. James Anderson, *Daily Life during the Spanish Inquisition* (Westport, CT: Greenwood Press, 2002), 182.

5. Anderson, *Daily Life during the Spanish Inquisition*, 184.

6. Juan Ruiz, *The Book of Good Love*, trans. Elizabeth Drayson MacDonald, ed. Melveena McKendrick (London: Everyman, 1999), 272, st. 1082, 1084–86.

7. Ruiz, *The Book of Good Love*, 273, st. 1082, 1084–86.

8. Ricardo Izquierdo Benito, *Abastecimiento y alimentación en Toledo en el siglo XV* (Cuenca: Ediciones de la Universidad de Castilla-La Mancha, 2002), 90.

9. Izquierdo Benito, *Abastecimiento y alimentación*, 89.

10. Tomás Puñal Fernández, *El Mercado en Madrid en la Baja Edad Media* (Madrid: Caja de Madrid, 1992), 196.

11. Puñal Fernández, *El Mercado en Madrid*, 103.

12. Izquierdo Benito, *Abastecimiento y alimentación*, 75.

13. Puñal Fernández, *El Mercado en Madrid*, 104.

14. Ruiz, *The Book of Good Love*, 272–74, st. 1088.

15. Ruiz, *The Book of Good Love*, 273–75, st. 1088.

16. Teófilo Ruiz, *Crisis and Continuity: Land and Town in Late Medieval Castile* (Philadelphia: University of Philadelphia Press, 1994), 77.

17. Izquierdo Benito, *Abastecimiento y alimentación*, 76.

18. Gitlitz and Davidson (*A Drizzle of Honey*) write that the removal of excess fat "recalls how the people of Israel used to make a sacrifice to God of the fat, throwing a piece of fat into the fire." The removal of the sciatic vein is "in remembrance of when the Angel fought with Jacob and he was left lame; and because of this the children of Israel do not eat the nerve in the leg nor the fat which is connected to it . . . as is written at the end of Genesis" (147).

19. Ibn al-Khatíb, *Libro de cuidado de la salud durante las estaciones del año o Libro de higiene*, trans. María de la Concepción Vazquez de Benito (Salamanca: Ediciones Universidad de Salamanca, 1984), 193.

20. Ibn al-Khatíb, *Libro de cuidado*, 199.

21. Ibn al-Khatíb, *Libro de cuidado*, 202.

22. Olivia Remie Constable, "Food and Meaning: Christian Understandings of Muslim Food and Food Ways in Spain, 1250–1550," *Viator* 44, no. 3 (2013): 210.

23. L. P. Harvey, *Muslims in Spain, 1500–1614* (Chicago: University of Chicago Press, 1990), 47.

24. Galo Sanchez, *El fuero de Madrid y los derechos locales castellanos* (Madrid: Ayuntamiento de Madrid, 1963), 47.

25. Pilar Léon Tello, "Disposiciones sobre judíos en los fueros de Castilla y León," *Medievalia* 8 (1989): 229.

26. Puñal Fernández, *El Mercado en Madrid*, 85.

27. Puñal Fernández, *El Mercado en Madrid*, 87.

28. Manuel Espadas Burgos, "Aspectos sociorreligiosos de la alimentación española," *Hispania* 35, no. 131 (1975): 549.

29. Puñal Fernández, *El Mercado en Madrid*, 93f.

30. Fabre-Vassas, *The Singular Beast*, 7.

31. Juan de Aviñon, *Sevillana Medicina* (Sevilla: Enrique Rasco, 1885), 112–14.

32. Moses Maimonides, *Medical Aphorisms Treatises 1–5*, trans. Gerrit Bos (Provo: Brigham Young University Press, 2004), 67.

33. Carolyn A. Nadeau, *Food Matters: Alonso Quijano's Diet and the Discourse of Early Modern Spain* (Toronto: University of Toronto Press, 2016), 13.

34. Ruberto de Nola, *Libro de cozina* (Barcelona: Paneuropea de Ediciones y Publicaciones, 1972), 62.

35. Ruiz, *The Book of Good Love*, 274, st. 1093.

36. Ruiz, *The Book of Good Love*, 175, st. 1093.

37. David Nirenberg, "Figures of Thought and Figures of Flesh: 'Jews' and 'Judaism' in Late-Medieval Spanish Poetry and Politics," *Speculum* 81, no. 2 (2006): 415.

38. Juan Alfredo Bellón, "Judíos y Conversos en el *Cancionero de Obras de Burlas Provocantes a Risa* (Valencia 1519)," *Miscelánea de estudios árabes y hebraicos*, no. 32 (1983): 143.

39. Nirenberg, "Figures of Thought and Figures of Flesh," 423.

40. Antón de Montoro, *Poesía completa*, ed. Marithelma Costa (Cleveland: Cleveland State University Press): 1990; quoted in Gitlitz and Davidson, *A Drizzle of Honey*, 164.

41. Quoted in Kenneth Scholberg, *Sátira e invectiva en la España medieval* (Madrid: Gredos, 1971), 352.

42. David M. Gitlitz, "Hybrid Conversos in the 'Libro Llamado el Alboraique.'" *Hispanic Review* 60 (1992): 7.

43. Quoted in Gitlitz, "Hybrid Conversos," 8.

44. Quoted in Elena Romero, "El olor del sábado: La adafina, del Arcipreste de Hita a las versiones 'light,'" in *La mesa puesta: Leyes, costumbres y recetas judías*, ed. Uriel Macías and Ricardo Izquierdo Benito (Cuenca: Ediciones de la Universidad de Castilla-La Mancha, 2010), 226.

45. Aviñon, *Sevillana Medicina*, 114.

46. Aviñon, *Sevillana Medicina*, 116.

47. Gitlitz and Davidson, *A Drizzle of Honey*, 109.

48. Joan Santanach, ed., *The Book of Sent Soví: Medieval Recipes from Catalonia*, trans. Robin Vogelzang (Barcelona: Barcino-Tamesis, 2014), 42–45.

49. Puñal Fernández, *El Mercado en Madrid*, 104–7.

50. Ruiz, *The Book of Good Love*, 272, line 1082c.

51. Ruiz, *The Book of Good Love*, 273, line 1086a.

52. Salvador López Quero, "El léxico gastronómico medieval del *Cancionero de Baena*," *Zeitschrift für romanische Philologie* 127, no. 3 (2011): 491.

53. Aviñon, *Sevillana Medicina*, 118.

54. See the story from Atlas Obscura: www.atlasobscura.com/articles/why-scared-animals-taste-worse.

55. Aviñon, *Sevillana Medicina*, 120–21.

56. Aviñon, *Sevillana Medicina*, 121.

57. Maimonides, *Medical Aphorisms Treatises*, 87.

58. Gitlitz and Davidson, *A Drizzle of Honey*, 75.

59. Aviñon, *Sevillana Medicina*, 122.

60. Al-Tugībī, *Relieves de las mesas*, 48.

61. Al-Tugībī, *Relieves de las mesas*, 49.

62. Gitlitz and Davidson, *A Drizzle of Honey*, 146.

63. Al-Tugībī, *Relieves de las mesas*, 42.

64. Santanach, *The Book of Sent Soví*, 123.

65. Santanach, *The Book of Sent Soví*, 215.

66. Gitlitz and Davidson, *A Drizzle of Honey*, 185.

67. Ruiz, *The Book of Good Love*, 272, lines 1084d–85a.

68. Pierre Bonnassie, Pierre Guichard, and Marie Claude Gerbet, *Las Españas Medievales*, trans. Bernat Hervas (Barcelona: Crítica Barcelona, 2001), 224.

69. Bonnassie et al., *Las Españas Medievales*, 226.

70. Joseph O'Callaghan, *A History of Medieval Spain* (Ithaca: Cornell University Press, 1983), 18.

71. Aviñon, *Sevillana Medicina*, 111.

72. Puñal Fernández, *El Mercado en Madrid*, 99.

73. López Quero, "El léxico gastronómico," 485.

74. Thomas Glick, *Islamic and Christian Spain in the Early Middle Ages* (Leiden: Brill, 2005), 105–6.

75. Gitlitz and Davidson, *A Drizzle of Honey*, 187.

76. Glick, *Islamic and Christian Spain*, 104.

77. Puñal Fernández, *El Mercado en Madrid*, 88.

78. Aviñon, *Sevillana Medicina*, 100–101.

79. Puñal Fernández, *El Mercado en Madrid*, 90.

80. Puñal Fernández, *El Mercado en Madrid*, 143–45.

81. Ruiz, *The Book of Good Love*, 294, 296 st. 1184cd–85.

82. Ruiz, *The Book of Good Love*, 295, 297, st. 1184cd–85.

83. Ruiz, *The Book of Good Love*, 302, st. 1218.

84. Ruiz, *The Book of Good Love*, 303, st. 1218.

85. Judah al-Harizi, *The Book of Tahkemoni: Jewish Tales from Medieval Spain*, trans. and ed. David Simha Segal (Portland: The Littman Library of Jewish Civilization, 2003), 202.

86. María Jesús Rubiera Mata, "La dieta de Ibn Quzmān: Notas sobre la alimentación andalusí a través de su literatura," in *La alimentación en las culturas islámicas: Una colección de estudios*, ed. Manuela Marín and David Waines (Madrid: Agencia Española de Cooperación Internacional, 1994), 128.

87. Rubiera Mata, "La dieta de Ibn Quzmān," 132.

88. Ibn Quzmān, *Cancionero andalusí*, ed. Federico Corriente (Madrid: Ediciones Hiperión, 1996), st. 8.0, 8.3, 67.

89. Remie Constable, "Food and Meaning," 217.

90. Expiración García Sánchez, "La alimentación de los andalusíes: Entre las normas médicas y la vida cotidiana," in *El Saber en al-Andalus. Textos y Estudios* 5, ed. Julia Maria Carabaza Bravo and Laila Carmen Mahmoud Makki Hornedo (Sevilla: Editorial Universidad de Sevilla, 2011), 126.

91. Gitlitz and Davidson, *A Drizzle of Honey*, 83.

92. Juan Cruz Cruz, ed., *Dietética medieval: Apéndice con la versión castellana del régimen de salud de Arnaldo de Vilanova* (Huesca: La Val de Onsera, 1997), 112.

93. Aviñon, *Sevillana Medicina*, 132.

94. Maimonides, *Medical Aphorisms Treatises*, 27.

95. Aviñon, *Sevillana Medicina*, 130.

96. Aviñon, *Sevillana Medicina*, 135.

97. Ruiz, *The Book of Good Love*, 276, lines 1103ab.

98. Ruiz, *The Book of Good Love*, 276, lines 1105ac.

99. Ruiz, *The Book of Good Love*, 278, lines 1106ab.

100. Ruiz, *The Book of Good Love*, 280, lines 1117abf.

101. Puñal Fernández, *El Mercado en Madrid*, 171.

102. Puñal Fernández, *El Mercado en Madrid*, 196.

103. Puñal Fernández, *El Mercado en Madrid*, 174.

104. Ruiz, *The Book of Good Love*, 303, st. 1216, 1219.

105. Ruiz, *The Book of Good Love*, 303, st. 1216, 1219.

106. C. M. Woolgar, "Food and Taste in Europe in the Middle Ages," in *Food: The History of Taste*, ed. Paul Freedman (London: Thames & Hudson, 2007), 165–66.

107. Bridget Ann Henisch, *Fast and Feast: Food in Medieval Society* (University Park: Penn State University Press, 1976), 31.

108. Ruiz, *The Book of Good Love*, 271, st. 1075.

109. Ruiz, *The Book of Good Love*, 271, st. 1075.

110. Ruiz, *The Book of Good Love*, 275, st. 1095.

111. Ruiz, *The Book of Good Love*, 275, st. 1095.

112. Ruiz, *The Book of Good Love*, 277, st. 1100.

113. Ruiz, *The Book of Good Love*, 277, st. 1100.

114. See Martha Daas, "Food for the Soul: Feasting and Fasting in the Spanish Middle Ages," *eHumanista* 25 (2013): 65–74, for more information on the meaning of Carnal's diet.

115. Francesc Eiximenis, *Francesc Eiximenis, An Anthology*, trans. Robert D. Hughes (Barcelona: Barcino-Tamesis, 2008), 159.

116. Alfonso Mártinez de Toledo, *Arcipreste de Talavera o Corbacho*, ed. Michael Gerli (Madrid: Cátedra, 1998), 130.

117. Terence Scully, *The Art of Cookery in the Middle Ages* (Woodbridge: The Boydell Press, 1995), 61.

118. Carolyn Walker Bynum, *Holy Feast and Holy Fast* (Berkeley: University of California Press, 1987), 38.

119. Walker Bynum, *Holy Feast and Holy Fast*, 41.

120. Scully, *The Art of Cookery in the Middle Ages*, 59.

121. Henisch, *Fast and Feast*, 39.

122. Walker Bynum, *Holy Feast and Holy Fast*, 42.

123. Mary Douglas, "Deciphering a Meal," in *Food and Culture: A Reader*, ed. Carole M. Counihan and Penny Van Esterik (London: Routledge, 1997), 54.

124. Richard A. Lobban Jr., "Pigs and Their Prohibition," *International Journal of Middle East Studies* 26, no. 1 (February 1994): 59.

125. www.jewishvirtuallibrary.org/vayikra-leviticus-chapter-11, v. 1–8.

126. quran.com/5.

127. David M. Freidenreich, *Foreigners and Their Food: Constructing Otherness in Jewish, Christian, and Islamic Law* (Berkeley: University of California Press, 2011), 133.

128. Freidenreich, *Foreigners and Their Food*, 105.

129. Espadas Burgos, "Aspectos sociorreligiosos," 550.

130. Freidenreich, *Foreigners and Their Food*, 112.

131. Freidenreich, *Foreigners and Their Food*, 40.

132. Muhammad Khalid Masud, "Food and the Notion of Purity in the Fatāwā Literature," in *La alimentación en las culturas Islámicas,* ed. Manuela Marín and David Waines (Madrid: Agencias Española de Cooperación Internacional, 1994), 107.

133. Freidenreich, *Foreigners and Their Food*, 96.

134. Petrus Alfonsi, *Dialogue against the Jews*, trans. Irven M. Resnick (Washington, DC: Catholic University of America Press, 2006), 53.

135. Alfonsi, *Dialogue against the Jews*, 268.

136. Andrés Bernáldez, *Historia de los Reyes Católicos Don Fernando y Doña Isabel* (Sevilla: Geofrin, 1870), 126.

137. David Raphael, *The Expulsion 1492 Chronicles* (North Hollywood: Carmi House Press, 1992), 63–64.

138. Luis Suárez Fernández, *The Expulsion of the Jews: A European Problem* (Barcelona: Ariel, 2012), 51.

139. James Amelang, *Parallel Histories: Muslims and Jews in Inquisitorial Spain* (Baton Rouge: Louisiana State University Press, 2013), 15.

140. Mary Elizabeth Perry, "Between Muslim and Christian Worlds: Moriscas and Identity in Early Modern Spain," *The Muslim World* 95 (2005): 185.

141. Perry, "Between Muslim and Christian Worlds," 186.

142. Amelang, *Parallel Histories*, 37.

143. Madera Allan, "Food Fight: Taste in the Inquisitorial Trials of Ciudad Real" (PhD dissertation, University of Pennsylvania, 2009), 34.

144. Allan, "Food Fight," 46.

145. Luis Martínez Kleiser, *Refranero general, ideológico español* (Madrid: Real Academia Española, 1953), 394–95.

146. Luis de Usoz y Río, *Cancionero de obras de burlas provocantes a risa* (Madrid, 1841), 89.

147. Bernáldez, *Historia de los Reyes Católicos*, 126.

148. Raphael, *The Expulsion 1492 Chronicles*, 64.

149. Remie Constable, "Food and Meaning," 221.

Chapter 2

Bread and Grains

In Berceo's miracle tale about Theophilus, the protagonist is accused of asking for better than wheat bread.[1] To go asking for "better than wheat bread" meant that one was looking for trouble and finding it. According to recipe books, religious manuals, and health handbooks, a hierarchy of grains existed, and nothing was finer than wheat flour. In today's market, barley, oats, and other hearty grains are prized among more health-conscious consumers. In the Middle Ages, most men and women had only ever tasted bread made of wheat flour during holy communion. Poorer breads were made of barley and rye. Only the rich could afford wheat on a regular basis.

Bread and grains were a constant source of worry in the fifteenth century. Bread made up much of the medieval diet: most well-fed men and women ate at least a pound of bread a day.[2] To earn your day's bread was to make a living. The kind of bread that was consumed could identify one's social status and religion. Wheat appears in the medieval dietetics manuals as the most desirable of grains. In Juan de Aviñon's *Sevillana Medicina* wheat bread is: "*la más ygual simiente que sea en el mundo para el cuerpo del ome, y el trigo es caliente en primer grado ygual entre humedad y sequedad*" (The most balanced grain for the human body that exists in the world, wheat is warm in the first degree and balanced in its moisture).[3] Unlike barley, which was considered cold and dry, wheat was warm and hovered somewhere between humid and dry. Like medical and faddish diets that we follow today, it is hard to determine how much of an influence these handbooks had on daily life in the Middle Ages. What we do know, however, is that much of this medical knowledge was also popular knowledge.

The hierarchy of grains existed for a variety of reasons: cultivation and production, humoral qualities, and religion. The cultivation of grains was one that varied throughout the regions. The arrival of the Muslims and their

innovations in agriculture led to a "green revolution" in Spain. This revolution led to permanent changes in systems of watering, crop rotation, and
the kinds of crops that were grown.[4] Depending on the quality of soil in a
particular region, wheat, barley, and rye were grown. Teófilo Ruiz points
out that in Segovia, rye was favored because of its moist soil, citing a rather
humorous stanza from *Libro de buen amor* (stanza 103) as proof of this fact.
A mountain girl outside of Segovia offers the archpriest rye bread, bad wine,
and salted meat in return for sexual favors.[5] In al-Andalus, however, there
was a constant shortage of wheat that worsened over time.[6]

One of the markers of Muslim use of land was the growth of "irrigation agriculture" or crops that required a false water source.[7] Glick calls the introduction
of irrigation the "*Noria* revolution"; the revolution of waterwheels (see figure
2.1). By the thirteenth century, there were said to be five thousand water wheels
on the Guadalquivir River.[8] Because of innovations in irrigation systems, Muslims were able to grow huge numbers of crops in once-arid lands. However,
Ruiz points out that the conservative north of Spain often rejected the innovations of the Muslims, maintaining the traditions of the earlier Middle Ages.[9]

Figure 2.1   Rueda de Alcantarilla, a waterwheel, first constructed in the fifteenth century. The current wheel dates to the 1950s. By Pedro J Pacheco.

Cultural differences between Muslims and Christians were marked not only by what food they ate but also by what was privileged as an agricultural staple and the processes by which these foods were grown. Yet wheat production seems to have been a crop that was prized by both Muslims and Christians. Glick writes that nomadic Muslim culture did not believe in the production of grain.[10] However, Manuela Marín identifies grains as the most important staple of the thirteenth-century urban elite diet in Muslim Spain, which demonstrates that urban Muslims maintained a diet that was similar to their fellow Christians and Jews.[11] Since grains were the cornerstone of the medieval diet, Ibn Wāfid, in his *Tratado de agricultura*, includes a long section on the specifics of building a granary and how to keep grain from harm. Suggestions include using a mixture of ash and wormwood and washing grains in vinegar to help prevent rot and bugs.[12]

The Muslim medical treatise titled *Kitāb al-Agdiya* by 'Abū-Marwān 'Abd al-Malik ibn Abī al-'Alā' ibn Zuhr (known as Avenzoar), the *Kulliyat* (known more commonly by the Latin name *Colliget*) by Averroes, and the *Régimen de Salud* by Maimonides discuss the properties of wheat and grain, relying on the Galenic properties of foodstuffs. According to Averroes, the healthiest bread was made by hand, with a leavening agent and wheat flour.[13] Maimonides argued for a diet based on whole grains, stating that refined flour was an unhealthy substitute. Further discussion in these manuals states that barley and rice were the best substitutes for wheat whereas millet, sorghum and rye were less desirable.[14]

Recipes for bread are seldom found in medieval Christian food manuals. However, the first chapter of Ibn Razīn's *Relieves de las mesas* contains five recipes for making bread. The recipes vary according to the way in which they are cooked (over a fire, in an oven, or in a clay pot), the kinds of grains used, and whether a leavening agent is added. The first recipe is a bread made from semolina. The recipe reads as follows:

Se coge sémola y se remoja, se le pone sal y se deja hasta que esté tierna; enton-ces se soba muy bien. Después se le pone levadura y se amasa poco a poco con agua, hasta que está a punto y se ve que está bien trabada. Después se le pone un poco de riqāq,[15] se mezcla con ello y se hacen obleas de la forma que se desee. Se pone dentro de un pañuelo de lino o de lana y se tapan con pieles de oveja o algo parecido. Se dejan hasta que suba la masa, lo que se sabe porque se destapa, se golpea con las manos y se oye un ruido. Después se cuecen en el horno mientras se vigila. Se limpian, se ponen en un recipiente y se consumen cuando se necesite.[16]

Take well-rinsed semolina and add salt and leave it until it is soft; then squeeze it out well. Add yeast and add water a little at a time until it feels and looks right. Add a little fine flour, mix together, and make loaves in the shape that you wish. Put the dough between a cloth of linen or wool and cover with sheepskin or something similar. Let the dough rise enough, which you will know once you uncover the dough and listen to the sound it makes when you hit it. Bake in an oven while you watch. Clean it and put it in a container to eat when needed.

As we can see, the recipe for bread has remained the same throughout history, even if the baking method has changed. The fifth bread recipe is for *pan de panizo* (millet bread). Sesame or anise seeds were used to top the bread. Accordingly, millet was considered the third most desirable grain in Muslim kitchens for bread after wheat and barley.[17]

Bread was consumed at every meal and, for most of the year, Muslims, Christians, and Jews ate the same bread. Avenzoar mentions eighteen varieties of bread consumed.[18] Unleavened bread marked Passover celebrations; however, some flatbreads were consumed by Muslims. Most urban households did not have their own ovens but used communal ovens in the town, which, according to James Anderson, were often owned by the Church or by the aristocracy (see figure 2.2).[19] Bread was made every day, or, like other foods, was bought at the market. Food production and consumption varied according to a city or country lifestyle. In rural settings, more people grew

Figure 2.2   Baking bread. *Source*: From the abridged Latinized MS Rome 4182 housed in the Biblioteca Casanatense in Rome, 1390–1400 (Cat. MS 4182), Tavv. 120.

their own food and slaughtered their own meat. Anderson writes that rye and barley were often turned into gruel or porridge rather than bread in households of the rural poor.[20]

Wheat production was highly profitable in the Middle Ages. Much of the wheat-producing lands were owned by larger monasteries, whose production went toward feeding those who lived within their own communities. Puñal Fernández writes that at the end of the fifteenth century, the lands around Madrid were producing much of the wheat needed for city dwellers. The processing of wheat employed many workers. The wheat, once reaped, was threshed and then taken by mule to be weighed and then milled. After the milling process, the wheat was weighed again and then sealed into containers to avoid tampering with the flour. The flour was then taken to the grain exchange or to private homes.[21]

Breadmaking was highly regulated in order to ensure purity of grain, weight, and size of the bread. Bread makers could pick up the flour at the exchange to take back to the ovens. Bread makers, mainly women, often sold the bread through their windows right out of the oven, although Madrid also maintained bread stalls in the marketplace.[22]

Markets were found both within city walls and outside the walls. Some were temporary but many became permanent. From the tradition of the *hisba* manual, we are able to glean much information about what kinds of grains were grown and sold in markets. There were a number of varieties of wheat sold in the markets including blond and red wheat, semolina, and wheat starch.[23] The sale of wheat was strictly regulated and, according to *hisba* manuals, any fraud was severely punished (see figure 2.3). Types of fraud perpetrated in the markets included the mixing of white powder or crushed bones into the wheat.[24]

Bread and grain were also used as a thickening agent for a variety of soups and stews. Both urban and rural people of the working class subsisted on a steady diet of vegetable stews made of legumes and bread or grains. The large number of recipes for soups and stews in collections of all three religions demonstrates their popularity. In Roberto de Nola's *Libro de cozina*, for example, there are more than ten recipes for "pottages." Also included in this collection is a recipe for the popular medieval dish known as "frumenty": a boiled grain dish made with milk, in this case almond milk, with added cinnamon and sugar.[25] The first chapter of *Relieves de las mesas* covers different recipes for not only bread but also soup with *migas*, which can be translated as crumbs or, more often in Arab cooking, couscous, then pottages of grains, then sweets made with grains (five, twenty-seven, eleven, and forty recipes, respectively). The final section of the grain portion of this text covers rice, couscous, and other savory dishes made with bulgur wheat (fourteen recipes). In Jewish recipes, *almidón* (starch made from wheat steeped in water) and

Figure 2.3 An illustration of the punishment dealt to bakers that had violated weight regulation on bread. The offender would be dragged through the city streets on a sled with the fraudulent bread tied around his neck. *Source*: City of Bristol Record Office.

rice flour were common.[26] Dishes made with crumbs sautéed in olive oil were also favored by Jewish cooks.

Aside from stews and other grain-based dishes, wheat and other flours were used for fritters and turnovers, which will be discussed further in chapter 4. In *The Book of Sent Soví,* there are a number of recipes for stuffed turnovers and fried fritters. The fact that these fritters were fried in pork fat marks this manual as Christian. Other fritters, like *buñuelos* or doughnuts, were fried in olive oil as they were traditionally found in Muslim cuisine. For Passover, honeyed fritters were a common treat. Gitlitz and Davidson write that these same fritters are eaten during Hanukkah by the Sephardic communities around the Mediterranean today.[27]

Couscous, rice, and pasta are some of the grains and grain-based comestibles that fill the pages of medieval cooking manuals (see figure 2.4). Remie Constable writes that "couscous came to be one of the most distinctive markers of cultural and culinary Islam by the late 15th century."[28] As late as the seventeenth century, one of the markers of the *morisco* population was their consumption of couscous, as can be attested to by the playwright Lope de Vega, who defined Muslims as "*gente que come arroz, pasas, higos, y alcuzcuz*" (people who eat rice, raisins, figs, and couscous).[29]

XXiv

Trij-

Naturic c.7b.m f.mettor cc cis. optete opciata uuuametu; pecron
7 gutun nocumetu;. uisenb;vebub; remotio nocumenti. cum
pzinoyo.

Figure 2.4 Pasta making. *Source*: From the abridged Latinized MS Rome 4182 housed in the Biblioteca Casanatense in Rome, 1390–1400 (Cat. MS 4182), fol. 84.

Chapter 5 of *Relieves de las mesas* is devoted to dishes that rely on soaked grains, crumbled breads, and noodles as the starch base. The recipes in this chapter range from the basic couscous and noodle recipes to complex stews made with beef or lamb, a variety of vegetables, and spices like pepper and cinnamon. Couscous was made of semolina. The dough was rubbed into small pieces, like the head of an ant, and then steamed, which remains the method of cooking couscous in traditional Middle Eastern cuisine.[30] Marín notes, *"La aportación más singular del Mágreb al repertorio gastronómico arabeislámico es alcuzcuz"* (The most important North African contribution to the Arabo-Islamic gastronomy is couscous).[31]

Couscous appears in Aldonza's culinary catalog in *La Lozana Andaluza*. Remie Constable points out that Aldonza's knowledge of how to cook couscous is what allows her entry into the expatriate community in Italy.[32] Most recipes for couscous appear in Muslim food manuals, whereas Christian and

Jewish recipes privileged rice. Rice can be seen as a steadfast staple in the medieval diet. Rice was grown in Iberia during the times of the Romans, and the Muslims brought the rice crops back to prominence. From the tenth century on, rice became an important crop in Iberia.[33]Antonio Gázquez Ortiz writes that the reputation of rice as an exotic food changed over the course of the fourteenth century into a staple of the Christian diet. Murcia, Castellón, and Valencia became the rice-producing areas in Spain. *Manjar blanco*, or *blancmange*, a common dish in the Middle Ages, was often made with rice.[34]

Rice was often used in a particularly popular Jewish dish called *adafina*. According to Gitlitz and Davidson, the name *adafina* was "derived from the Arabic term for 'hidden,' since the pot's cover, which helped retain the heat, hid the contents from view."[35] *Adafina* was a dish that could be made on Friday to serve to the family during the Sabbath. It was also the cause of many accusations by the Holy Office.[36] This common stew appears in a number of literary references and Inquisition transcripts. Bernáldez wrote of the converted Jews: "*Nunca perdieron el comer a costumbre judáica de manjarejos é olletas de afinas*" (They never lost the Jewish custom of eating *adafina*").[37] The Sabbath stew also appears in the *Cancionero*: "*Trobar en nunca comer/ lo del Rabí devedado/sino manjar trasnochado*" (Sing of refusing to eat what the Rabbi has forbidden but eat the Sabbath stew).[38] The word *trasnochado* means to be kept overnight in Spanish and is one of the many names for this dish.[39] The poet, like Bernáldez, accuses the converted Jews of maintaining their rituals, including their food customs.

Inquisition trial testimonies often mentioned foods and preparation rituals. The testimony of a witness in the trial of Juan González Pintado specifically mentions *adafina* as a suspicious food. González Pintado had been secretary to two kings, Juan II and Enrique IV, but, as history shows, political power often did nothing to protect someone from unwanted attention of the Holy Office. His trial took place in 1483–1484 in Ciudad Real. A witness claims: "*E que otra vegada le dieron a comer de vna cosa que era guisada con muchas espeçias, e que dezian que era adafina, e que ove que aquel pan blanco que comió que era pan çençeño*" (And another time they gave him something to eat that was a stew with many spices and they called it *adafina*, and the bread that he ate was unleavened bread).[40] According to the trial testimony, González Pintado was not guilty of many "sins" against Christianity, yet he was found guilty and burned at the end of February 1484.[41]

In the trial of Juan de Chinchilla, alias Juan Soga, he and his wife, Sancha Gonçales, were seen cooking on a Friday to keep for Saturday and lighting clean candles ("*guisauan de comer el viernes para el sabado e ençendian los candiles lympios*").[42] The common stews called alternatively *adafina*, *trasnochado*, or *boronía* could be found at many tables in the Middle Ages.

These same stews, by the end of the fifteenth century, had been turned into a powerful weapon of accusation against converted Jews.

The history of pasta in Iberian Peninsula can be traced back to the Romans. Pasta, however, is not often associated with the Iberian Middle Ages. Surprisingly, Muslim food manuals contain a number of recipes that call for noodles. The Spanish word *fideos* comes from the Arabic word *fidawš*.[43] In *Relieves de las mesas,* there are recipes for *fideos*, which are small, thin noodles that have been dried in the sun and then boiled. Another noodle is called *al-muhammis*, which has not entered the Spanish lexicon. According to Marín, this noodle was made into small rounds and then dried, like the thin *fideos*. A third kind of noodle, called *aletría*, which comes from the Arabic *al-itrīya* (angel hair pasta), is formed on a long table, making it *"lo más fina que se pueda"* (the thinnest possible) and then allowing the noodles to dry in the sun.[44] And finally, a dish called *al-taltin*, which has entered the lexicon as *tallarines* (*tagliatelle*)—these are much wider noodles, cut ¨*del ancho de dos dedos*¨ (the width of two fingers) that are also dried in the sun.[45] Although many of the noodle dishes are eaten with meat and vegetables, the noodles themselves seem to be adorned only with salt and butter, an odd twist to the olive-oil rich recipes in the text.

There is no mention in the collection compiled by Gitlitz and Davidson of noodles, so the assumption is that rice was the main starch served with stews. We do find noodles mentioned in Nola's food manual. His recipe for *Potaje de fideos* calls for almond milk, like the frumenty mentioned earlier. Carolyn Nadeau points out that this may be Nola's sensitivity to Jewish traditions of not mixing meat and dairy.[46] The consumption of rice, couscous, and pasta is complicated by the tie between ethnicity and religion. These side dishes became more or less popular depending upon the level of tolerance found in particular communities.

BREAD AND GRAINS IN LITERATURE

In the literature of medieval Iberia wheat maintains an important religious association because of its connection with Christian communion. Throughout Christian texts of the Middle Ages, bread was a metaphor for Christ. Bread is both the humble Christian repast and a powerfully transformative element. It represents both the penitent meal and the meal of enlightenment. Caroline Walker Bynum writes that from the very beginning, "the eucharistic elements stood primarily not for nature, for grain and grape, but for human beings bound into community by commensality."[47] Both eating and abstaining from eating embody powerful spiritual choices. Christ, challenged by the devil to transform a stone into bread to relieve his hunger, chose instead to abstain (Matthew 4:1–4):

> Then Jesus was led up by the Spirit into the wilderness to be tempted by the devil. He fasted forty days and forty nights, and afterwards he was famished. The tempter came and said to him, "If you are the Son of God, command these stones to become loaves of bread." But he answered, "It is written, 'One does not live by bread alone, but by every word that comes from the mouth of God.'"[48]

Adam and Eve, however, transgress God's will in the Garden of Eden precisely through the act of eating (Genesis 3:6): "So when the woman saw that the tree was good for food, and that it was a delight to the eyes, and that the tree was to be desired to make one wise, she took of its fruit and ate; and she also gave some to her husband, who was with her, and he ate."[49]

Eating represents a material temptation, which leads the sinner to commit more spiritual sins. However, man is also redeemed through an act of eating. By the end of the twelfth century, the word *transubstantiation* was widely used although its concept had been accepted as an informal tenet much earlier. The Fourth Lateran Council, in its first canon, declared the truth of *transsubstantiatio*:

> In which there is the same priest and sacrifice, Jesus Christ, whose body and blood are truly contained in the sacrament of the altar under the forms of bread and wine; the bread being changed *(transsubstantiatio)* by divine power into the body, and the wine into the blood, so that to realize the mystery of unity we may receive of Him what He has received of us.[50]

The host, then, as the holiest of foodstuffs, could only be made with the finest grain, which, in the Middle Ages, meant wheat.

The importance of wheat figures officially in Alfonso X's *Siete Partidas.* Law 52 of part I states: "The bread, which is called the Host, must be made of wheat flour."[51] In his *Sacrificio de la Misa*, Berceo writes,

Aún del Corpus Dómini   *otra cosa vos digo,*
El pan de que se faze   *deve seer de trigo;*
otra mezcla ninguna   *no la quiere consigo:*
yo esto bien lo creo   *e só ende testigo.*

Si se buelve en ello   *nulla otra cevera,*
esto atal se finca   *tal pan qual ante era;*
el trigo sólo torna   *en carne verdadera,*
la que mete las almas   *en buena carrera.*[52]

I will tell you still more about *Corpus Domini*
the bread it is made of must come from wheat;
it must not be mixed with anything else;
I witness to this and I firmly believe it.

If any other grain is mixed with it,
such bread will stay just as it was;
only wheat becomes the true flesh
that places souls on the right path.[53]

The association of Christ with wheat and, thus, the host, becomes much more literal after the doctrine of transubstantiation. Christ appears in many literary texts as wheat or wheat bread. The Virgin Mary, then, appears as both the mother of wheat bread and the oven in which the bread is baked.

These two images make a striking appearance in the tale of "*El judezno*" ("The Little Jewish Boy"), which is part of Berceo's collection of Marian miracle tales. Like all of the stories in this collection, "El judezno" is a version of an exemplum that existed for hundreds of years. Miri Rubin traces the origin of the tale in both Greek and Latin to the sixth century, although there are multiple medieval incarnations of the tale.[54] The story tells of a little Jewish boy who goes to mass with his Christian friends on Easter Sunday. The text reads:

En el día de Pascua,   domingo grand mañana,
quando van Corpus Domini   prender la yent christiana,
priso'l al judezno   de comulgar grand gana,
comulgó con los otros   el cordero sin lana.

Mientre que comulgavan   a muy grand presura
el ninno judezno   alzó la catadura,
vio sobre'l altar   una bella figura,
una fermosa duenna   con genta creatura.[55]

On Easter Sunday, very early in the morning,
when the Christian people go to take Corpus Domini,
a great desire to commune seized the little Jewish boy.
The wool-less lamb took Communion with the others.

While they were taking Communion with very great zeal,
the little Jewish boy raised his gaze;
he saw over the altar a lovely figure,
a beautiful lady with a lovely Child.[56]

When the boy returns home, he confesses that he has partaken of the Eucharist. The boy's father, convinced that the boy is a traitor to the family and its religion, punishes him by throwing him into an oven. However, because of the transformative power of the Eucharist, the boy is now considered a Christian and therefore worthy of the Virgin Mary's attention. She protects him from the flames and then encourages the crowd to avenge the boy by throwing the father into the oven. Miri Rubin writes that ovens are rich in connotations and eucharistic meaning; they were "both life-denying and food-giving."[57] One of the last stanzas of the tale reads:

Tal es Sancta María   que es de gracia plena,
por servicio da Gloria,   por deservicio pena;
a los bonos da trigo,   a los malos avena,
los unos van en Gloria,   los otros en cadena.[58]

Such is Holy Mary, who is full of grace;
for service she gives glory, for disservice punishment;
to the good she gives wheat, to the evil oats;
the good go to glory, the others go in chains.[59]

The desirable grain, wheat, is associated with goodness, whereas an undesirable grain, like oats, is associated with evil.

Since Christ is ostensibly wheat bread, to go looking for better than wheat bread, like our poor Theophilus did in the stanza quoted in the beginning of the chapter, was to sin. After selling his soul to the devil, Theophilus is accused of having asked for better than wheat bread (*demandar mejor de pan de trigo*).[60] For his penance, Theophilus first must abstain from both food and drink for three days in order to prepare for his transformation from grave sinner to penitent Christian. Stanza 895 reads:

Adiesso que Teófilo,   un cuerpo martiriado,
reçibió Corpus Domini   e fue bien confessado,
fue a ojo del pueblo   de claridad cercado,
un resplandor tan fiero   que non serié asmado.[61]

As soon as Theophilus, a mortified body,
received Corpus Domini and was fully confessed,
he was surrounded by brightness within the sight of the people,
a splendor so great it could not be imagined.[62]

The transformative power of the Eucharist and the witnessing of this power allows Theophilus to become a full-fledged member of the Christian community again.

Not only is wheat the holiest of grains, but bread made from wheat was mainly for those who could afford the expensive grain. A poor, but saintly man in another miracle tale, "*El pobre caritativo*," ("The Charitable Pauper"), is promised by the Virgin Mary that he will receive the finest food in heaven. In this case, it happens to be bread made of *trigo candeal*, the best wheat bread.[63] There is, according to the Virgin, no finer food, as it is the most superior bread, surely never before eaten by a poor man, and also representative of Christ himself.

Many of Ibn Quzmān's *zéjeles* mention the consumption of wheat and bread or bemoan the lack of this most basic of food groups. In *zéjel* 16, verse 4, the poet laments his poverty:

Si en la casa harina pones, se sigue lo demás,
y esas cosas sólo quiero tras la saciedad;
pascua es y no tengo harina ni dinero,
preciso harina y dinero para gastar;
por mi gusto, si pudiera, ahogaría a esta miseria.[64]

If you give me flour, the rest will follow.
and I only want these other things after I am satisfied;
it is the holiday and I have neither flour nor money,
I need flour and money to spend;
so that my pleasure may drown this misery.

And also in *zéjel* 67 verse 14:

Ojalá en casa tanta harina hubiera como bocados me faltan,
porque me haría unos puches, si hubiera gota de aceite;
pero tampoco hay leña: cuanto me falta he nombrado,
que si tuviera un mendrugo, bien que me lo tostaría.[65]

If I only had some flour, since I am starving,
because I would make some pottage, if I had a drop of olive oil;
but there is also no firewood; I have named what I need,
and if I had a crust, I would surely keep it.

In the Jewish tradition, wheat was also highly prized (see figure 2.5). There was little difference in the bread eaten by Jews except during Passover when *matzo*, or unleavened bread was consumed. The tradition of *matzo*, however, caused problems in the later Middle Ages because of Christian prejudice. Marc Michael Epstein notes that Jews were suspected of "reliving the crucifixion" by stealing pieces of the Eucharist and profaning it (see figure 2.6). By its very nature as unleavened bread, Christian theologians believed that *matzo* was a Jewish imitation of the Eucharist.[66]

Figure 2.5   Detail of a page: Historiated initial-word panel "Ha lahma aniya" ("The Bread of Affliction"), at the beginning of the text of the Haggadah. Beneath the initial words, a miniature depicting a family by the Seder table with the master of the house placing the basket of unleavened bread on the head of one of his children. *Source:* Haggadah, *Liturgical Poems and Biblical Readings for Passover*, the Barcelona Haggadah, c. 1340.

Inquisition trial notes make a number of references to the consumption of *"pan çençeño"* or unleavened bread. In the Trial of Juan de Chinchilla, alias Juan Soga, he and his wife are accused of celebrating Passover: *"E sabe e vido que guardauan la Pascua del Pan Çençeño, e lo hazian e lo comian en su casa"* (and he knows and saw that they celebrated Passover and they made it and ate in in their house).[67] The "it" in this case is the unleavened bread. The importance of "seeing" and "knowing" are key to understanding the trial notes. As in the miracle tales, the power of the witness emphasizes the truth of the matter.

The poor in the Middle Ages, like the poor man in the Marian miracle, would not generally have had the chance to eat much wheat bread. For them, barley, rye, and millet were the most common grains for bread and mashes. Medieval literature abounds with negative references to barley, rye, and oats. In one poem of the *Cancionero de obras de burlas provocantes de risa*, the horse complains that he is fed barley while his owner is fed wheat.[68]

Figure 2.6 A Medieval painting depicting host desecration by Jews. The stories of Jews desecrating the host were some of the more troubling myths that were passed around multiple countries and communities in the Middle Ages. By the fourteenth century, as the importance of the Eucharist grew, so too did paranoia of its desecration. *Source*: Museu Nacional d'Art de Catalunya.

In Berceo's collection of miracle tales barley bread makes an appearance in the tale of "*La abadesa preñada*" ("The Pregnant Abbess"). In this tale, an abbess finds herself pregnant after straying into sin. She is such a devoted servant to Mary, however, that the Virgin comes to her aid not only by taking the child away to be adopted by a holy hermit, but also by erasing any sign of her pregnancy.

Quando se sintió delivre   la prennada mesquina
fo el saco vaçío   de la mala farina,
empezó con gran gozo   cantar "Salve Regina,"
que es de los cuitados   solaz e medicina.[69]

When the poor pregnant one felt herself delivered,
the sack emptied of the bad flour,

with great joy she began to sing, "Salve Regina"
the solace and medicine of the afflicted.[70]

The child is unwanted and therefore described as *"mala farina"* (bad flour).
The description of the abbess's sinful pregnancy stands in stark contrast to
the Christ child who is made of the finest wheat.

The tale continues with a description of the anger the nuns harbored toward
their abbess, reporting her to the bishop. Berceo writes, *"Fizieron su cabillo
la ira e el odio,/amasaron su massa de farina de ordio"*[71] ("Anger and hatred
had their meeting; they kneaded their dough with barley flour"[72]). Although
barley flour was considered second best according to medieval manuals, it is
still far inferior to the Christ-like wheat flour. Richard Terry Mount writes
that inferior bread was associated with punishments in the monasteries.[73]

In Berceo's *Vida de Santo Domingo de Silos* (*The Life of Saint Dominic
of Silos*), the poet tells of a woman possessed by the devil. She goes to the
monastery to pray for a miracle: *"Yogo ant el sepulcro toda una semana,/
comiendo pan de ordio, con vestidos de lana"*[74] (For one whole week she lay
before the tomb,/eating barley[75] bread and dressed in wool clothing"[76]). In
this text barley bread is part of the woman's penance and directly contrasts
the Christ-like wheat bread. Oats also make a rare appearance in this text.
The Saint is captured by "Moors" and put into chains. The text tells us that
he is so hungry that he would willingly eat bread made of oats, which were
considered horse fodder and rarely found in the dishes of medieval Iberia.

Metiéronlo en fierros   e en dura cadena,
de lazrar e famne   dávanli fiera pena;
dávanli yantar mala   e non buena la çena,
combrié, si gelo diessen,   de grado pan davena.[77]

They put him in irons and on a heavy chain;
they caused him dreadful anguish in suffering and hunger;
he was fed a rotten lunch and an even worse supper;
had they given him oat bread he would have gladly eaten it.[78]

Hannele Klemettilä writes that ants, in the second-century bestiary, the
Physiologus, which was popular in the Middle Ages, "recognized barley and
rye as cattle fodder by their smell and thus collected only wheat."[79] Rye, even
more than barley, was considered a poor substitution for blessed wheat. Rye
bread is mentioned in *Libro de buen amor* as a source of humor and distress
for our poor archpriest. While crossing the mountains, the archpriest, starving
and cold, is saved by a lusty mountain girl. She provides shelter and a meal:

diome pan de çenteno,
tyznado, moreno,
e dion vino malo,
agrillo e Ralo,
e carne salada.[80]

She gave me rye bread,
dark and blackened,
gave me bad wine,
bitter and thin,
and salt meat.[81]

The scene is a parody of the *locus amoenus* trope. Instead of a paradise on earth, the archpriest finds himself in a compromising position with a woman whose ears are bigger than a donkey's and a nose like a curlew's beak, all for the sake of a terrible meal.

Barley makes an appearance in Ibn Quzmān's *zéjeles*, although in a more positive light. In *zéjel* 67, verse 12 he writes:

Pardiez, que la harina es cara, y el comer, más que perfume,
y la mayoría divide la cebada a dedo y uña;
la Sanjuanada ha llegado, como ves, y es fiesta ésta
no de presumir de ropa, sino de pan en la tabla.[82]

Lord, but flour is expensive, and to eat it is dearer than perfume,
and most people count the barley grains one by one.
The festival of San Juan has arrived, as you see, and it is a party
not to show off your clothes, but rather to have bread to eat.

The poet's poverty allows him to be less than picky in his choice of grains. For him, bread is bread, regardless of its origins. By examining these writings, we can see that only in Christianity is there a necessary link between holiness and wheat.

RELIGIOUS IMPLICATIONS

Walker Bynum writes that the meaning of food and hunger changed in the Middle Ages: hunger meant human vulnerability, which God comforted with food, or it meant human self-control, adopted in an effort to keep God's commandments. To eat God was to become suffering flesh, it was to imitate the cross.[83] No poem more aptly describes the phenomenon of suffering flesh better than the poem of Saint Mary of Egypt, known in the Escorial MS.h.I.13 as *María Egiçiaca.* Mary the Egyptian spends the first half of her life living intemperately. She is guilty of consuming all the pleasures of life: *"Todo su cuydado era de bien comer e de bien beuer e de ser sienpre en luxuria"* (All she cared about was eating well and drinking well and sexual pleasures).[84] However, she has a change of heart that leads her to a life of abstinence and penance. She begins her new life by entering the desert with the most basic of foods: three breads. These breads are loaded with meaning: they are the penitent's most basic repast; they are Mary's only sustenance for years, and they represent the Eucharistic meal. For her, the scarcity of food and the harshness of the desert strip her of her gluttonous fleshly desires. Penance at this time generally took the form of abstinence from all comforts: food, drink, sex, and soft living. This extreme of penance, however, was often looked upon as suspicious, bordering on the heretical. Yet the life of Mary of Egypt provided a context for penance that could not just be tolerated, but admired and imitated.

Although bread was the most common of foodstuffs in the Middle Ages, consumption rituals and religious rites marked differences among Christians, Muslims, and Jews. While making *matzo,* the custom existed of pinching off a small piece of the risen dough and throwing it into the fire before baking in memory of the sacrifice of the people of Israel.[85] Since communal ovens were often used in the Middle Ages to bake bread, Jewish women had to find "sympathetic" ovens to be able to bake the *matzo.*[86]

Eating unleavened bread was one of the Judaizing customs mentioned in the Edicts of Grace published by the Inquisition. These edicts "enumerated heretical practices and announced a set period during which sinners could confess their participation in the proscribed activities, repent and be reconciled to the Church."[87] These customs could only be observed by close friends, neighbors, and, of course, servants. Inquisition trials brought to a head the suspicion of "the other" in Spanish society. Grievances, both perceived and otherwise, could be avenged simply by reporting on one's friend, neighbor, master, or mistress. Inquisition trial notes are filled with reports by snooping neighbors and servants on the consumption of Sabbath stews and suspiciously unleavened bread. Unlike the unleavened bread eaten by the Jewish population of Iberia during Passover, the Muslims were not accustomed to eating different bread than the Christians. What marked Muslim habits was the consumption of grains like couscous and the making of fried fritters known as *buñuelos.*

Remie Constable tells us that a number of laws established by Queen Catalina, mother of Juan II, in 1412 spoke to the conflation of religion and food practices. Specifically, Muslims were "forbidden from selling bread, butter, or anything edible to Christians. . . . Nor should Muslims visit Christians or send them gifts of spices, baked bread, poultry, nor any other killed meat, or dead fish, or fruits, or . . . anything else to eat."[88] A thirteenth-century statute from Avignon reads, "Jews and prostitutes may not dare to touch with their hands bread or fruit displayed for sale; those who do so must purchase that which they touched or grasped."[89] Commensality, then, became an avenue through which one could be "contaminated" by the other's religion. Freidenreich reminds us that "biblical dietary laws neither segregate nor differentiate Us from Them. They classify foodstuffs, not people, and play no direct role in maintaining proper order."[90] On the other hand, Madera Allan writes that the legislation against the sharing of food between Jews and Christians was "redundant," considering that "sharing meals with practicants of other religions had been forbidden since at least the Talmudic era."[91] Since both Christians and Jews felt it necessary to reiterate their prohibitions, Allan writes that it is likely that commensality between the two religions was common.[92]

Why, then, did Christian laws from the thirteenth century prohibit not only the breaking of bread together but commerce of foodstuffs between members of different religions? In order to create an us-versus-them mentality, common habits needed to be marked as "foreign" or "other." The most basic of these is consumption habits. Christians, in their push toward religious domination of the peninsula, saw commensality as a path toward a "contamination" of religion.

Miri Rubin writes, "Just as the eucharist's power was emphasised and increasingly realised, the myriad dangers and mishaps which could befall the host became clear."[93] The narrative of host desecration became more popular after the Fourth Lateran Council and grew in popularity and ferocity throughout the centuries. As a political and propagandistic anti-Semitic tool, a variety of literary genres were used to spread the rumors. Rubin writes that poems, plays, chronicles, and exempla were used to bring the mythology of desecration alive.[94]

This fear of pollution of one's religion is palpable in the texts of the later Middle Ages. As Jewish converts to Christianity grew in number in the fifteenth century, tales of host desecration grew in intensity.[95] Freidenreich writes,

> Jewish, Christian and Islamic authorities employ similar scholastic modes of thinking, imagined conceptions of foreigners, and techniques of textual interpretation. These similarities are even greater among those who live in a common intellectual culture (Christian Europe or Islamic Near East).[96]

Yet these shared modes of thinking are not compatible with the systematic dominance of a culture or religion. The concepts of "Old" Christian and "New" Christian played out in a variety of ways. The "converso" or converted Jew or Muslim was held to a different standard. There are a number of examples in popular literature that mock conversos with food imagery.

Some of these relate to the host desecration, while others accuse converts of falling into old habits of eating *adafina* and couscous. Regardless of the commensality that existed earlier in the Middle Ages, by the fifteenth century, anti-Jewish and anti-Muslim sentiments became part of the fabric of society.

NOTES

1. Gonzalo de Berceo, "The Miracle of Theophilus," in *The Collected Works of Gonzalo de Berceo*, trans. Jeannie K. Bartha, Annette Grant Cash, and Richard Terry Mount (Tempe: Arizona Center for Medieval and Renaissance Studies, 2008), 129, l. 804c.

2. Juan de Aviñon, *Sevillana Medicina* (Sevilla: Enrique Rasco, 1885), 51.

3. Aviñon, *Sevillana Medicina*, 62.

4. Thomas Glick, *Islamic and Christian Spain in the Early Middle Ages* (Leiden: Brill, 2005), 75.

5. Teófilo Ruiz, *Crisis and Continuity: Land and Town in Late Medieval Castile* (Philadelphia: University of Pennsylvania Press, 1994), 92.

6. Glick, *Islamic and Christian Spain in the Early Middle Ages*, 82.

7. Glick, *Islamic and Christian Spain in the Early Middle Ages*, 75.

8. Glick, *Islamic and Christian Spain in the Early Middle Ages*, 75.

9. Ruiz, *Crisis and Continuity*, 96.

10. Glick, *Islamic and Christian Spain in the Early Middle Ages*, 82.

11. Ibn Razīn al-Tugībī, *Relieves de las mesas, acerca de las delicias de la comida y los diferentes platos*, ed. and trans. Manuel Marín (Gijón, Spain: Ediciones Trea, 2007), 30.

12. 'Abd al-Rahmān ibn Muhammad ibn Wāfid, *Tratado de agricultura*, trans. Cipriano Cuadrado Romero (Málaga: Analecta Malacitana, 1997), 91.

13. Expiración García Sánchez, "La alimentación popular urbana en al-Andalus," *Arqueología medieval* 4, (1996): 223.

14. Jordi Salas-Salvado, "Diet and Dietetics in al-Andalus," *British Journal of Nutrition* 96, suppl. 1 (2006): s103.

15. Marín (in al-Tugībī, *Relieves de las mesas*) writes that *riqāq* is a type of thin, unleavened bread. In this recipe, however (citing F. de la Granja: *La cocina arábigo-andaluza*), she believes that it refers to a fine wheat flour (77n11).

16. al-Tugībī, *Relieves de las mesas*, 77–78.

17. al-Tugībī, *Relieves de las mesas*, 79n16.

18. García Sánchez, "La alimentación popular urbana," 224.

19. James Anderson, *Daily Life during the Spanish Inquisition* (Westport, CT: Greenwood Press, 2002), 188.

20. Anderson, *Daily Life during the Spanish Inquisition*, 188.

21. Tomás Puñal Fernández, *El Mercado en Madrid en la Baja Edad Media* (Madrid: Caja de Madrid, 1992), 39.

22. Puñal Fernández, *El Mercado en Madrid*, 40.

23. García Sánchez, "La alimentación popular urbana," 223.

24. García Sánchez, "La alimentación popular urbana," 224.

25. Ruberto de Nola, *Libro de cozina* (Barcelona: Paneuropea de Ediciones y Publicaciones, 1972), 83.

26. David M. Gitlitz and Linda Kay Davidson, *A Drizzle of Honey: The Lives and Recipes of Spain's Secret Jews* (New York: St. Martin's Press, 1999), 16.

27. Gitlitz and Davidson, *A Drizzle of Honey*, 270.

28. Olivia Remie Constable, "Food and Meaning: Christian Understandings of Muslim Food and Food Ways in Spain, 1250–1550," *Viator* 44, no. 3 (2013): 213.

29. Antonio Crespo, "'Los Porceles de Murcia,' comedia de Lope de Vega." *Revista Murgetana*, no. 109 (2003): 78.

30. al-Tugībī, *Relieves de las mesas*, 130.

31. al-Tugībī, *Relieves de las mesas*, 130n81.

32. Remie Constable, "Food and Meaning," 214.

33. Pierre Bonnassie, Pierre Guichard, and Marie Claude Gerbet, *Las Españas Medievales*, trans. Bernat Hervas (Barcelona: Crítica Barcelona, 2001), 139.

34. Antonio Gázquez Ortiz, *La cocina en tiempos del Arcipreste de Hita* (Madrid: Alianza Editorial, 2002), 101.

35. Gitlitz and Davidson, *A Drizzle of Honey*, 148.

36. Manuel Espadas Burgos, "Aspectos sociorreligiosos de la alimentación española," *Hispania* 35, no. 131 (1975): 552.

37. Andrés Bernáldez, *Historia de los Reyes Católicos Don Fernando y Doña Isabel* (Sevilla: Geofrin, 1870), 126.

38. Luis de Usoz y Río, *Cancionero de obras de burlas provocantes a risa* (Madrid, 1841), 90.

39. Gitlitz and Davidson, *A Drizzle of Honey*, 148.

40. Haim Beinart, *Los conversos ante el Tribunal de la Inquisición* (Barcelona: Riopiedras Ediciones, 1983), 115.

41. Haim Beinart, *Records of the Trials of the Spanish Inquisition in Ciudad Real, Volume One: The Trials of 1483–1485* (Jerusalem: The Israel Academy of Sciences and Humanities, 1974), 93–94.

42. Beinart, *Los conversos*, 174.

43. García Sánchez, "La alimentación popular urbana," 226.

44. al-Tugībī, *Relieves de las mesas*, 135.

45. al-Tugībī, *Relieves de las mesas*, 137.

46. Carolyn A. Nadeau, *Food Matters: Alonso Quijano's Diet and the Discourse of Early Modern Spain* (Toronto: University of Toronto Press, 2016), 122.

47. Caroline Walker Bynum, *Holy Feast and Holy Fast* (Berkeley: University of California Press, 1987), 48.

48. www.biblegateway.com/passage/?search=Matthew+1–4&version=NRSV.

49. www.biblegateway.com/passage/?search=Genesis+3–6&version=NRSV.

50. https://sourcebooks.fordham.edu/basis/lateran4.asp.

51. King Alfonso X, *Las Siete Partidas, Volume I*, trans. Samuel Parsons Scott (Philadelphia: University Pennsylvania Press, 2001), 39.

52. Gonzalo de Berceo, "Del Sacrificio de la Misa," in *Obra Completa*, ed. B. Dutton et al. (Madrid: Espasa-Calpe, 1992), 1002–3, st. 172–73.

53. Gonzalo de Berceo, "The Sacrifice of the Mass," in *The Collected Works of Gonzalo de Berceo*, trans. Jeannie K. Bartha, Annette Grant Cash, and Richard Terry Mount (Tempe: Arizona Center for Medieval and Renaissance Studies, 2008) 459, st. 172–73.

54. Miri Rubin, *Gentile Tales: The Narrative Assault on Late Medieval Jews* (New Haven: Yale University Press, 1999), 8.

55. Gonzalo de Berceo, *Milagros de Nuestra Señora*, ed. Michael Gerli (Madrid: Cátedra, 1988), 133, st. 356–57.

56. Gonzalo de Berceo, "Los Milagros de Nuestra Señora," in *The Collected Works of Gonzalo de Berceo*, trans. Jeannie K. Bartha, Annette Grant Cash, and Richard Terry Mount (Tempe: Arizona Center for Medieval and Renaissance Studies, 2008), 69, st. 356–57.

57. Rubin, *Gentile Tales*, 25.

58. Berceo, *Milagros,* 135–36, st. 374.

59. Berceo, *The Collected Works of Gonzalo de Berceo*, trans. Jeannie K. Bartha, Annette Grant Cash, and Richard Terry Mount (Tempe: Arizona Center for Medieval and Renaissance Studies, 2008), 72, st. 374.

60. Berceo, *Milagros*, 203, l. 804c.

61. Berceo, *Milagros*, 216, st. 895.

62. Berceo, *The Collected Works*, 139, st. 895.

63. Berceo, *Milagros*, 95, l. 137c.

64. Ibn Quzmān, *Cancionero andalusí*, ed. Federico Corriente (Madrid: Ediciones Hiperión, 1996), 90.

65. Ibn Quzmān, *Cancionero andalusí*, 192.

66. Marc Michael Epstein, "Birds' Head Haggadah—Scholar Gives New Insights into Jewish Medieval Text," Medievalists.net, April 2012, www.medievalists.net /2012/04/birds-head-haggadah-scholar-gives-new-insights-into-jewish-medieval-text.

67. Beinart, *Los conversos*, 174.

68. Usoz y Río, *Cancionero de obras*, 93.

69. Berceo*, Milagros*, 162, st. 539.

70. Berceo, *The Collected Works*, 95, st. 539.

71. Berceo, *Milagros*, 164, ll. 552cd.

72. Berceo, *The Collected Works*, 97, ll. 552cd.

73. Richard Terry Mount, "Levels of Meaning: Grains, Bread, and Bread Making as Informative Images in Berceo," *Hispania* 76, no. 1 (1993): 51.

74. Berceo, *The Collected Works*, 431, ll. 689ab.

75. Bartha translates *pan de ordio* as "oat bread," but "*ordio*" is barley.

76. Berceo, *The Collected Works*, 306, ll. 689ab.

77. Berceo, *Obra completa*, 347, st. 355.

78. Berceo, *The Collected Works*, 266, st. 355.

79. Hannele Klemettilä, *The Medieval Kitchen* (London: Reaktion Books Ltd., 2012), 148.

80. Juan Ruiz, *The Book of Good Love*, trans. Elizabeth Drayson MacDonald, ed. Melveena McKendrick (London: Everyman, 1999), 256, st. 1030.

81. Ruiz, *The Book of Good Love*, 257, st. 1030.

82. Ibn Quzmān, *Cancionero andalusí*, 191.

83. Walker Bynum, *Holy Feast and Holy Fast*, 54.

84. John K. Moore Jr., *Libro de los huéspedes (Escorial MS h.I.13): A Critical Edition* (Tempe: Arizona Center for Medieval and Renaissance Studies, 2008), 26.

85. Gitlitz and Davidson, *A Drizzle of Honey*, 242–43.

86. Madera Allan, "Food Fight: Taste in the Inquisitorial Trials of Ciudad Real" (PhD dissertation, University of Pennsylvania, 2009), 31.

87. Madera Allan, "An Elusive Minimal Pair: Taste and Caste in Inquisitorial La Mancha," *Ehumanista* 25 (2013): 97.

88. Remie Constable, "Food and Meaning," 208.

89. David M. Freidenreich, *Foreigners and Their Food: Constructing Otherness in Jewish, Christian, and Islamic Law* (Berkeley: University of California Press, 2011), 194n37.

90. Freidenreich, *Foreigners and Their Food*, 38.

91. Allan, "Food Fight," 27.

92. Allan, "Food Fight," 27.

93. Rubin, *Gentile Tales*, 29.

94. Rubin, *Gentile Tales*, 134–35.

95. Rubin, *Gentile Tales*, 98.

96. Freidenreich, *Foreigners and Their Food*, 224.

Chapter 3

Vegetables and Legumes

In the second volume of *Don Quijote*, Sancho Panza makes the following observation: "*Por la mayor parte, he oído que los moros son amigos de berenjenas*" (Generally, I have heard that the Moors are great fans of eggplant).[1] To be called an "eggplant eater" (*berenjenero*) was a terrible insult in the fifteenth century.[2] Commonly found in Jewish and Muslim dishes, eggplants became a marker of the *converso* or Christian convert. With the Green Revolution came an explosion of a variety of vegetables in the medieval Iberian diet. Eggplant was just one of the many vegetables introduced by the Arabs. Other crops included artichokes, carrots, spinach, nuts, as well as rice, citrus fruits, and sugar cane.[3] Olive trees had been part of the landscape since Phoenician times, but the proliferation of the use of olive oil grew under Muslim dominion of agriculture. Legumes too became a staple of the diets of Christians, Muslims, and Jews. Garbanzos and lentils provided affordable nourishment to much of the population.

The popularity of spices increased as their importance grew in the market. "The purpose of spices was fourfold: to change the nature of the dish in humoral terms; to alter its flavor; to dictate its color; and to indicate the standing of the establishment in terms of conspicuous consumption."[4] Onions and garlic were already staples of Iberian cuisine, but the Arabs brought a number of other spices to the table including cilantro, cumin, cinnamon, ginger, saffron, and pepper. Spices, however, were considered a luxury and were not found in the households of the poor.[5]

Carolyn Nadeau writes that "most, if not all vegetables cut across socio-economic boundaries."[6] However, heavily vegetarian diets were certainly more common among the poor and for religious ascetics. The abstention of meat in the monastic diet was not only associated with sexual abstinence, but also, in some cases, with the desire to follow an

Edenic diet, that is, "a nonviolent alimentary model that avoided killing living creatures."[7] For the poor, meat was a luxury that could only be purchased or produced in small quantities. The staples of the poor included artichokes, turnips, beans, garlic, onions, olives, cheese, and bread.[8] The diets of Muslims and *moriscos* also tended toward a heavier use of vegetables and legumes.

Today's reader would be astonished by the numbers of vegetables eaten in medieval Iberia. When we picture medieval diets, generally what comes to mind is meat, bread, and an odd root vegetable or two. The remnants of the Visigothic diet can be seen in the farming habits of northern Iberia during the Middle Ages. Much of the land was devoted to grains (wheat, barley, and rye), viticulture, and dairy. Georges Duby writes, "The *demesne*, therefore, was cereal-growing by tradition, viticultural by the lord's inclination, and pastoral by financial interest."[9]

The differences in the crops between the north and the south can be attributed to both culture and climate. In the Christian north, the old traditional rotation of two crops per year followed by a fallow period allowed for a less varied production that included grains like wheat, rye, barley, and millet, and vegetable crops like turnips, onions, garlic, and cabbage. García Sánchez writes that vineyards covered much of the north, but the rich olive production remained in Al-Andalus.[10] The Green Revolution, brought about by Muslim agricultural techniques, did not necessarily take hold in the northern reaches of Iberia. In Al-Andalus, the watering technology and the science of crop rotation created an agriculture that provided fruits and vegetables throughout the year (see figure 3.1). García Sánchez elaborates,

Los andalusíes podían consumir verduras y hortalizas frescas casi todo el año— las de verano: calabaza, berenjenas, judías, sandía, pepinos, melón y ajos que se recolectaban hasta el mes de octubre rotaban con las de invierno: nabo, col, zanahoria, acelga, puerros, etc, que aparecían a partir de noviembre.[11]

The people of Al-Andalus were able to eat leafy greens and vegetables almost the entire year: the crops of the summer include gourds, eggplant, green beans, watermelon, cucumbers, melon, and garlic. These were harvested until October. Winter crops include turnips, cabbage, carrots, chard, leeks and were harvested starting in November.

García Sánchez differentiates between *verduras* and *hortalizas*. In the 1611 dictionary titled *Tesoro de la lengua castellana o española* by Sebastián Covarrubias, *verdura* and *hortaliza* seem to be interchangeable:

HORTALIZA, lo que fe coge de fruta en la huerta, y fe cria en las heras (tierras) della como rauano, lechuga, y col, etc.

Figure 3.1 **A scene of agricultural work with a man digging herbaceous plants with a spade, among cultivated trees.** *Source*: From a Medieval Arabic manuscript from Al-Andalus (Islamic Spain).

What can be picked from the orchard or grown in the ground like radishes, lettuce, and cabbage, etc.[12]

VERDVRA, lo que está verde: pero comúnmente se toma por las legumbres que se crían en las huertas como lechugas, rauanos, etc.

Green vegetables that are grown in orchards like lettuce, radishes, etc.[13]

The other classification of green in the cooking and medical manuals is *hierbas* (herbs). In Covarrubias the definition takes an entire page and covers all manner of uses including medicinal and culinary. The basic definition reads:

IERVA: Todo lo que cria la tierra de fuyo, que no tiene mas q hojas fin tallo, fe llama yerba. Yervas fuelen llamarfe las legumbres que fe crian en los huertos, que fe echan en la olla, y hazen también enfalada dellas.[14]

Everything that grows from the ground that only has leaves, without a stalk, is
called an herb. Herbs are grown in gardens and are used to season and to make
salads.

The Real Academia Española defines *hierba* as: *"Toda planta pequeña
cuyo tallo es tierno y perece después de dar la simiente en el mismo año, o a
lo más al segundo, a diferencia de las matas, arbustos y árboles, que echan
troncos o tallos duros y leñosos"* (All small plants whose stalk is tender and
dies after its first or, at the most, its second flowering, differing from all kinds
of bushes and trees that have trunks or hard stalks).[15] The *hortaliza* is defined
as an edible plant that is grown in a garden or orchard and a *verdura* is an
edible plant with green leaves. In both agricultural texts and food manuals,
the terms *verdura*, *hortaliza*, and *hierba* are often used interchangeably.

Ibn Wāfid's *Tratado de agricultura* outlines the monthly schedule for
agricultural activities. For example, in late January and February legumes
and vines should be planted.[16] The text also gives recommendations for the
different kinds of soil in which each vegetable should be planted. Beans and
garbanzos, advises Ibn Wāfid, should be planted in damp soil.[17] Leeks, on the
other hand, should be grown in sandy soil.[18]

El Calendario de Córdoba outlines not only the months in which vegetables and legumes should be cultivated, but also the times in which wild plants
can be found. In February, for example, one can find truffles, fennel, and
asparagus.[19] The *Calendario* confirms the timeline for the legumes, planted
in February and harvested in the summer. In March, cucumbers and eggplants
should be planted as well as sunflowers.[20] In April, one may sow basil, cau-
liflowers, green beans, and cucumbers.[21] In June medicinal plants are picked
and cabbages are planted.[22] In July herbs like mustard, nigella, and thyme are
picked.[23] In October, olives are beginning to be ready to be harvested.[24] In
November, summer vegetables are gone, but winter vegetables, like cabbage,
turnips, carrots, radishes, leeks, and chard are abundant.[25]

The variety of produce available depended on a number of factors, but the
most important was location. The residents of the area now known as Andalucía were able to enjoy a wider variety of foodstuffs because of the weather
and the crop rotation style introduced by the Muslims. Most people also
maintained a small kitchen garden for personal use. In these small gardens
they would grow onions, garlic, turnips, carrots, and other hearty vegetables.
There are few references to the growing of legumes, although we know
through the *Tratado de Agricultura* and the *Calendario de Córdoba,* that
these products were indeed grown for general consumption.

There were a number of ways that people could obtain what they could
not grow for themselves. Foraging was a very common activity. One could

find asparagus, artichokes, mushrooms, acorns, and other foods in the forests. Foraging also happened in fields that were already harvested, which was not considered illegal. Stealing, however, was common. Teresa de Castro Martínez writes that people often took advantage of holy days and Sundays, as well as late evening hours to sneak into orchards and fields to steal a wide variety of products including almonds, olives, melons, and garbanzos. The most expensive foods, like dates and almonds, would have been stolen for resale in a kind of medieval black market.[26]

In general, the resale of food products was prohibited. People who bought at bargain prices and resold often undercut the actual sellers. However, there were few rules about who could sell their vegetables in the open market. Vegetables were not as regulated as other foodstuffs.[27]

Olives were one of the most prevalent and lucrative crops grown in the Iberian Peninsula. According to Glick, olives were a staple of Hispano-Roman agriculture.[28] Spain today relies heavily on olive oil for cooking. However, in the Middle Ages, the use of olive oil was controversial. Remie Constable writes that inquisitors "peered into new Christian frying pans" to ascertain if olive oil had been used instead of lard.[29]

Lard was considered the appropriate fat to use in Christian cooking. Olive oil was used almost exclusively by Muslims and Jews in their cooking. Abū Marwān Abd Al-Malik ibn Zuhr, in his treaty on food from the twelfth century, categorizes olive oil as a perfectly balanced food, humorally speaking.[30] Although one of Bernáldez's complaints was that Jewish homes smelled bad because of their use of olive oil when frying meats, during Lent, when animal products were forbidden, Christians too cooked with olive oil. Jews also used olive oil to light their synagogue lamps. Gitlitz and Davidson write that "dozens of Inquisition cases from the years just prior to the expulsions testify to the crypto-Jewish custom of donating oil for synagogue lamps."[31] Replacing olive trees with fields of wheat became a symbol of Christian domination over Muslim lands. Glick writes that wheat tithes became more valuable than olive oil tithes by the end of the thirteenth century.[32] However, olives remained a popular crop in *morisco*-dominated regions.

Like olives, legumes were a staple of the medieval diet, although recipes that featured them were scarce. The legumes that appear in the *Sevillana Medicina* are beans, lentils, and chickpeas. According to the health handbook, they should be consumed according to their humoral properties. Beans are cold and wet: they are good for the chest, but cause gas. Juan de Aviñon points out that beans prepared during Lent are good for cooling the stomach.[33] Foods that engender "coolness" were considered appropriate during Lent since they were known to dampen sexual ardor.

Lentils are cold and dry and produce melancholy, so they should be eaten sparingly. Ibn Wāfid recommends eating lentils with vinegar to make them more palatable and to reduce the sadness that their consumption inevitably brings.[34] Aviñon does point out that lentils are excellent for ill people because they cool fevers and fight against "rot."[35] Garbanzos have many more positive properties and uses than the aforementioned legumes. Aviñon identifies two kinds of garbanzos: white and brown. White garbanzos are warm and humid and are used to fill out a meal, to add leavening like yeast, and to improve constipation, kidney stones, and intestinal worms. They also help to bring on menses. The brown garbanzos are used primarily for medicinal purposes. The brown garbanzos were often used to make a stew for ill people.[36]

Chapter 14 of the *Sevillana Medicina* devotes twelve pages to the properties of vegetables consumed in the fifteenth century. The vegetables listed include onions, garlic, eggplant, gourds, carrots, cucumbers, a variety of greens including parsley, cilantro, chard, and endive, leeks, artichokes, turnips, radishes, asparagus, mushrooms (including truffles), and cabbage. Although there are a few exceptions, most vegetables fall into two humoral categories: cold and wet or warm and dry. As one can imagine, most greens and watery vegetables are cold and wet. Generally, the cooler vegetables are good to eat raw, especially lettuce, with vinegar, to cool the stomach and increase the appetite.

Radishes occupy an entire page of the manual with heightened warnings against their poor properties, including the fact that they produce terrible nausea.[37] Indeed, Ibn Quzmān wrote a tongue-in-cheek poem titled "The Radish" in which he calls the vegetable "a powerful repeater."[38] Asparagus and carrots fare well in the book, as they are warm, dry, and very nutritious. They both help with menses and allow for urine to flow freely. Apparently, eggplants are less nutritious, but Aviñon points out that treating them with salt and then rinsing them will give them a more healthful outlook. He also suggests cooking eggplant with meat. Aviñon cites both Persian and Muslim medical authorities in the section on eggplant. Aviñon writes that both Rasis and Abenrruyz (Averroes) recommend eggplant for their nutritive value.[39] "Rasis" refers to Abū Bakr Muhammad Zakariyyā Rāzī, a Persian scholar who lived between the years 854–925 and was one of the first scholars to use humoral theory. Maimonides also recommends eggplant for stomach ailments. Other vegetables that maintain positive properties, according to Maimonides, are spinach for pleurisy; asparagus for backaches caused by wind; and turnips for nursing mothers.[40]

Onions fare poorly in Aviñon as they engender bad humors, give one bad breath, produce gas, and generally cause melancholy and terrifying dreams. However, they serve a medicinal purpose in that they produce blood flow and urine flow and arouse both physical and sexual appetites. Leeks supposedly heighten sex drive, while garlic is good for phlegmatics but bad for cholerics because it warms the blood. However, according to "country folk," garlic counteracts poisons, which definitely is a quality in its favor (see figure 3.2).[41]

Figure 3.2 Harvesting garlic. *Source*: From the *Tacuinum sanitatis* (fifteenth century).

Aviñon dedicates the rest of the *Yervas* chapter to herbs and spices. After garlic and onions, Aviñon mentions cilantro, purslane, ginger, cumin, caraway, fennel, mint, aniseed, cinnamon, mustard seed, and salt. In this section, Aviñon again refers to Averroes and al-Rāzī, but also mentions "Ipocrás" (Hippocrates) and "Isac." Isac refers to Isac Israeli ben Solomon, a Jewish philosopher and physician born in Cairo and who served a number of North African rulers in the tenth century. He wrote a medical treatise on fevers (*Kitāb al-Ḥummayat*, *The Book of Fevers*, in Hebrew *Sefer ha-Ḳadaḥot*). Aviñon writes, "*Dize Isac que mezclado con vinagre [el culantro] amansa la calentura del estómago*" (Isaac says that cilantro mixed with vinegar calms a heated stomach).[42] The cool and wet herbs like cilantro and purslane are good for stomach ailments and fevers. Maimonides recommends oregano for vision problems, anise for cleansing the uterus, and dill for hiccups.[43] Other spices that are warm and dry, like cumin, fennel, caraway, ginger, and cinnamon help with stomach ailments, swelling and also make meat taste better.[44] The last entry in this chapter discusses the merits of salt. According to Aviñon, salt aids digestion, helps balance the humors of phlegmatics, and adds flavor to meat.[45]

The variety of vegetables represented in *Relieves de las mesas* gives us a good understanding of the popularity of specific vegetables at the time. The king of the Muslim vegetable empire was the eggplant. Other popular vegetables were "*calabaza*," which can be understood as a squashlike gourd, spinach and other leafy greens, artichokes, asparagus, and cauliflower. Marín reminds us that there are many chapters missing from the cookbook, which would give us an even better idea of the importance of certain vegetables (like mushrooms).[46]

The first chapter in the vegetable section is devoted to *calabaza vinatera*, the calabash, or bottle gourd, with eleven recipes (see figure 3.3). To prepare the gourd in the first recipe, first it must be peeled and cleaned. Then it is cooked in salted water. Once it is cooked, the gourd is taken out of the water and allowed to drain. Then the recipe calls for the vegetable to be dipped in flour and fried in oil until golden. The fried gourd is mixed with cilantro, fried *migas* (breadcrumbs), almonds, and egg.[47] Some of the recipes call for a mixture of onions, garlic, and almonds or pine nuts to go with the cooked gourd.[48] *Migas*, eggs,

Figure 3.3 Squash was one of the most common and versatile vegetables used in Arab cooking. *Source*: From the *Tacuinum sanitatis*, Vienna MS 2644, housed in the Osterreichische Nationalbibliothek, 1390–1400.

and cilantro are also common to many of the recipes. Interestingly, there is no mention of mixing the gourds with meat.

An entire chapter in *Relieves* is devoted to eggplant (twenty-two recipes).[49] To prepare eggplant, the recipes call for peeling and boiling the eggplant and then discarding that liquid. However, each recipe varies in its ingredients: many are made with ground meat; others are made into casseroles or frittatas. Some dishes also call for honey to be mixed in with eggplant.[50]

Eggplants make an appearance in Nola's *Libro de cozina*, the aforementioned *"berengenas a la Morisca"* (eggplant in the Morisco style)[51] and in the *The Book of Sent Soví,* mixed with onion, parsley, mint, and marjoram.[52] Eggplants were also an important part of Jewish cooking. Jewish recipes often called for stuffing eggplants with lamb or making them into a frittata. Gitlitz and Davidson write that the *"fritada"* was popular because of its flexibility but was always made with eggs and cheese.[53] The same recipe can be found in Muslim and Christian food manuals (the recipe in the *Sent Soví* is indeed a casserole). However, casseroles cooked by *converso* families were considered suspicious by the Inquisition because they could be eaten cold on the Sabbath.[54]

The tradition of the frittata, which allows for any vegetable to be included, demonstrates the common usage of a number of different greens. Multiple recipes included in *A Drizzle of Honey* call for chard: both as part of cold dishes and also boiled and fried. Gitlitz and Davidson cite a satirical poem from the collection *Cancionero de Baena* in which Rodrigo Cota describes a converso wedding at which guests were served eggplants and chard, but no pork or fish without scales:

En la boda desta aljama
no se comió peliagudo
ni pescado sin escama
en quanto 'l marido pudo;
sino mucha verengena
y açafrán con alçelguilla.
Quien "¡Jesu!" diga en la çena,
que no coma albondiguilla.

At this Jewish wedding party
Bristly pig was not consumed;
Not one single scaleless fish
Went down the gullet of the groom;
Instead, an eggplant casserole
with saffron and Swiss chard;
And whoever swore by "Jesus"
From the meatball pot was barred.[55]

In Nola's *Libro de cozina,* the recipes call for fewer vegetables (mainly spinach and onions), but he puts herbs and spices to liberal use. The most commonly mentioned herbs are parsley, mint, cilantro, and garlic. Spices include salt, pepper, ginger, cinnamon, saffron, cloves, and nutmeg.

Legumes are mostly absent in Christian cooking manuals. Nola's book has one recipe for *"hava real"* or fava beans, which can be found in the section identified as Lenten foods. The beans are cooked in almond milk, although the author writes that goat's milk is preferable.[56] In the *Manual de mugeres,* chickpeas make one appearance in an aptly named *"olla morisca"* (Moorish stew), made up of goat, onions, mutton, spices, and chickpeas. Fava beans are more common in Jewish recipes. Gitlitz and Davidson include a variety of recipes that call for fava beans and chickpeas. They write that chickpeas were "pervasive" in converso cooking.[57] One recipe titled "Blanca Ramírez's Chickpeas and Bean Stew" calls for both legumes plus beef or lamb. The spices include coriander, cumin and caraway, and chard is added near the end.[58] Other Sabbath stews, like *adafina,* also called for a combination of chickpeas and beans.[59]

Marín points out that there are only three kinds of legumes mentioned in *Relieves de las mesas*: garbanzos, fava or broad beans, and lentils. Of the three, garbanzos are found in the majority of these recipes. In fact, lentils play little to no role in the cookbook, which, according to Marín, is an oddity. She posits that lentils may not have been part of the larger diet of the Muslim elite, which corresponds to the idea that lentils were indeed "poor food."[60]

VEGETABLES AND LEGUMES IN LITERATURE

Lentils, although a common element of abstinence diets, were traditionally associated with the diets of the lower classes. A medieval lament of a poor Jew reads:

Lechuga el domingo
Migajas y agua el lunes.
Puerros el martes.
Las sobras de los puerros el miércoles.
Lentejas secas el jueves
Los restos de las lentejas el viernes.
Mientras que en sabat lo más prudente es no cenar.
Ni mucha carne, ni mucho vino.

Lettuce on Sundays
Bread and water on Mondays
Leeks on Tuesdays

Leek leftovers on Wednesdays.
Dry lentils on Thursdays
The rest of the lentils on Fridays.
While on the Sabbath, not dining is the most prudent of all.
Not much meat, nor much wine.[61]

Vegetables and legumes figure heavily in *Libro de buen amor*. The iconic battle of Lady Lent and Lord Carnal and the subsequent punishment of Carnal contextualizes the medieval attitude toward vegetables and legumes. Although it is pure satire, it is not hard to see that Ruiz's treatment of these foodstuffs might reflect general feelings of the time.

The first stanza of the section on the battle between Lent and Carnal reads:

Acercando sse viene vn tiempo de dios santo,
fffuy me para mi tierra por folgar algund quanto,
dende a siete dias era quaresma tanto,
puso por todo el mundo miedo e grand espanto.[62]

One of God's holy times approached,
and I returned home to rest awhile.
There were only seven days till Lent
and everyone was fearful and worried.[63]

Carnal hopes to avoid the battle, but the Church's calendar is a foregone conclusion. Lent will prevail for forty days. Although as we saw in chapter 2, Lady Lent relies heavily on her fishy troops, vegetables do also play a role in the battle. Indeed, the first blow is made by the leek:

El primero de todos que ferio a don carnal
fue el puerro cuelle aluo e ferio lo muy mal
fizole escopir flema, esta fue grand Señal,
tovo doña quaresma que era suyo el Real.[64]

The very first to wound Carnal
was the white-necked leek; he dealt a nasty blow
and made Carnal spit phlegm—it was a significant sign,
for Lent believed the camp was hers.[65]

This stanza is ripe with humor and sexual innuendo. According to the *Sevillana medicina,* leeks heighten one's sexual appetites (see figure 3.4).[66] Carnal spitting phlegm is an obvious reference to ejaculation.

Reeling from his defeat at the hands of Lady Lent, our poor Lord Carnal must then be subjected to a diet that is both Lenten in nature and also designed to cool his choleric temperament. On Sunday for his covetousness,

Figure 3.4   Leeks were well known in the Middle Ages for a number of good properties including the ability to stimulate the sexual appetite. *Source*: From the *Tacuinum sanitatis*, Vienna MS 2644, housed in the Osterreichische Nationalbibliothek, 1390–1400.

he must eat chickpeas cooked in oil; Monday he is to eat peas to combat his pride; on Wednesday he is prescribed spinach to cool his lust; Thursday calls for lentils to tame his ire; and on Saturday he must eat beans for his envy. Carnal's diet resonates medically and ecclesiastically. Spinach, as a cold and wet vegetable, would be good for anyone of a choleric nature. The chickpeas were to be cooked in oil, demonstrating that lard was forbidden during Lent. Legumes were also prescribed for those of a sanguine nature. According to Vilanova, lentils *"amenguan la sangre y rebajan la ira y el arrebatamiento"* (lentils cool the blood and reduce one's anger and excitement).[67]

An allegorical depiction of nature's bounty can also be found in *Libro de buen amor*. Lord Love awaits those who seek his counsel at the end of the Lenten season. The Lord's tent is an ekphrastic depiction of the harvests and its seasons. The visitors to Lord Love's tent represent the seasons and the foods that are commonly harvested or planted during those particular months. Barbara Kurtz writes that the seasons are not only represented by the kinds of foods that are available, but also, metaphorically, by different groups of people. The winter, for example, is represented by knights. Since knights have nothing to do with agricultural labor, winter is fitting as there is really no labor to be done in the fields.[68] In the winter stanzas (1272–75), root vegetables like parsnips and carrots are eaten and fed to working animals; sowing corn and roasting chestnuts as well as salting meats and clarifying wine with chalk are all mentioned.

In early spring, represented by *hidalgos*, or noblemen, we see the business of pruning and grafting vines for the grape harvest.[69] Another nobleman plants cuttings of olive branches "*que dan aseyte bueno*" (to give good oil).[70] Summer, represented by "*ricos hombres*" (rich men), represents the bounty of the harvest. The first was in charge of ripening corn and fruit and lunches on goat's liver and rhubarb.[71] He also searches for herbs in the mountains.[72] The second reaps fodder and eats early figs and rice.[73] Autumn, represented by farmworkers, sees them eating ripe grapes and figs and treading the grapes to prepare wine for the long winter.[74] Kurtz writes that this visualization of the calendar allows a panorama of rural Castile.[75]

Ibn Quzmān mentions a variety of vegetables and legumes in his poetry, albeit not as commonly as he writes of his desire for finer foods. In one poem, Ibn Quzmān eats *baqal* to cure a hangover. *Baqal*, according to Rubiera Mata, is a word that can mean both legume and vegetable.[76] *Mutallat*, which is a typical vegetable stew found in both Jewish and Muslim cuisine, also makes an appearance in *zéjel* 19, verse 5:

Trajo la mesa y acercó el candil,
poniéndome un poco de mutallat,
y dijo: "Señor, ha traído el mayoral
unos duraznillos y granada zafarí."[77]

He set the table and brought me a candle,
serving me a little bit of *mutallat*,
and said, "Master, the overseer has brought
these little peaches and also a wild pomegranate."

Corriente Córdoba notes that *mutallat*, in this context, is a poor man's soup.[78] A recipe for *mutallat* can also be found in *Relieves de las mesas* made with eggplant, gourd, onion, and garlic.

The appearance of a fava bean finds love in some Arab poetry of the eleventh century. Abū-l-Hasan ibn ʿAlī writes:

Engaste de marfil cuya caja es de jade
Encierra lo negro que adorna su rostro: como un ojo que tuviera
  una mancha negra.
Se la escoge fresca o seca y su delicioso perfume encanta al alma.[79]

Mounted in ivory, whose box is made of jade.
It encloses the darkness that adorns its face like an iris with a black stain.
Eaten fresh or dried, its delicious scent enchants the soul.

And Abū 'Amir ibn Suhayd writes that the fava bean is "the food of the courtly man, food of the scholar, beloved of all who are cultured and well educated."[80] Artichokes, too, make a lovely subject for many Andalusian poets. They are compared to hedgehogs, armor, and darts strong enough to pierce an elephant's hide.[81]

The emigré Aldonza, from Delicado's *La lozana andaluza*, lists a number of vegetables and legumes in her nostalgic memory of eating in Granada. In her *morisco* kitchen, couscous was cooked with garbanzos, turnips cooked with cumin (but without salt pork), Murcian cabbages with caraway seeds, stewed eggplants and eggplant casseroles, and dried fish stew with bigger greens.[82]

The fifteenth-century *Cancionero de burlas* satirizes false converts who consume suspicious foods:

Trobád vuestros dineros
con razones no muy flacas,
lindos garbanzos cocheros
y jentiles espinacas . . .

Trobád en pláticas buenas
Por estas tales pasadas,
En culantro y berengenas,
Y castañas adobadas.[83]

Sing about your stacks of money,
make your rhymes out of your riches,
sing of chickpeas, fat and sunny,
and of tasty spinach dishes . . .

Sing of good conversations
In those times past,
Of cilantro and eggplants
and marinated chestnuts.

The foods that suspected false converts consume like chickpeas, spinach, and eggplants are conflated with the stereotypical notion of the Jew as money lender or financier. Other questionable activities mentioned in the poem include keeping the Sabbath and avoiding eels and rabbit.

Foods such as eggplants, artichokes, fava beans, and spinach were sung about lovingly in the eleventh century and dreamed about nostalgically in exile in the sixteenth. These foods were considered staples of the Iberian diet of the Middle Ages. Yet, in the fifteenth century, they were marked as "*cosas viles*"—vile things, consumed by vile people who chose to ignore the "truth" of Christianity.

HERBS AND SPICES

Spices maintain an interesting position in the medieval diet; they are considered both heavenly and devilish. The Garden of Eden was perfumed with a heady mixture of spices. Yet moralists in the twelfth and thirteenth centuries warned against the aphrodisiacal and gluttonous nature of too much spice. Paul Freedman writes that the tradition of cooking with spices predated the Muslim arrival in Iberia. He notes that in the sole surviving Roman cookbook, 80 percent of the recipes call for pepper.[84] There can be no doubt, however, that the connection between the Muslim domination of the spice trade in the Middle Ages and the Muslim rulers of Iberia led to an increase in the importation of spices.

The use of spices depended more on one's financial well-being than on the religion one practiced. The prices of spices were exorbitant, which led to a second avenue of disdain by the moralists of the time. Freedman writes that the price of a pound of ginger "remained steady at an average of three and one-half times a carpenter's daily wages, while cloves rose from five to six times those wages."[85] By examining commercial accounts in Barcelona in the fourteenth century, Freedman gives us a general list of the prices of spices. For example, pepper cost 5 sous per pound, whereas saffron, always the most expensive of culinary spices even though it was grown in country, cost 80 sous (see figure 3.5). Spices used for medicinal purposes could be even higher. Camphor, also found on Freedman's list, cost 176 sous.[86]

Fraudulent practices abounded in the selling of spices. Like the fraud perpetrated in the selling of wheat with ground-up bones, Freedman writes that adulterated spices were often sold in markets and led to serious punishments, including death (see figure 3.6).[87] *Hisba* manuals and *fueros* warned against the sale of fake saffron.[88]

In recipes of all three religions, a wide variety of spices was used. Spices were considered a staple at most tables and were used as much for taste as for health. Spices were known to "harmonize the humors."[89] Gitlitz and Davidson write that "spices did not attract the attention of the Inquisition like particular foods did."[90] Out of 200 recipes in Nola's cookbook, 154 called for sugar, 125 required cinnamon, and 76 ginger.[91] In *Relieves de las mesas*, some of the most common spices include saffron, cumin, cinnamon, ginger, and pepper, mastic, cloves, cardamom, galangal, bay leaves, celery seed, and

Crœbus.

Crœbus oplo ca . ι. fic. mp. Electio oziul ui rubc. oueial. uuuui. lenficar coz ι ο fciz egre
bio. fii. uecuñi. faer nauseñ. Remõ uaeñi ñi fuco auomioz aut uino aen ꝺoufcro. Oꝺ gnir
ſanguiñe lonum ſbrilé aenri miſ uciz. fii. ſembi rcuic a ſeptentrionalibi.

Figure 3.5   Saffron (Crocus). *Source*: From the *Tacuinum sanitatis*, Vienna MS 2644, housed in the Osterreichische Nationalbibliothek, 1390–1400.

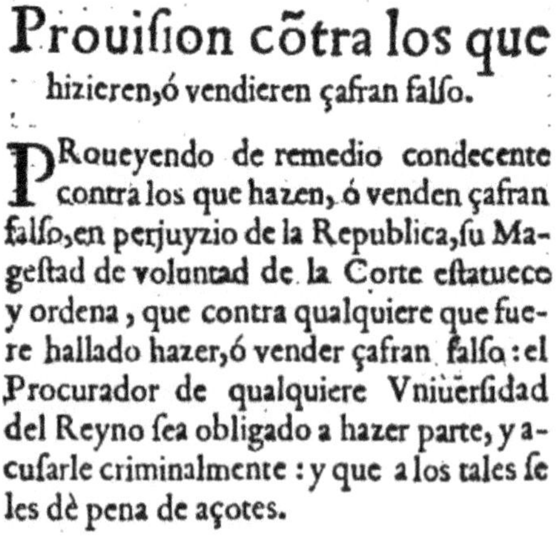

Prouifion cõtra los que
hizieren,ó vendieren çafran falſo.

PRoueyendo de remedio condecente
contra los que hazen, ó venden çafran
falſo,en perjuyzio de la Republica,ſu Ma-
geſtad de voluntad de la Corte eſtatueco
y ordena , que contra qualquiere que fue-
re hallado hazer,ó vender çafran falſo : el
Procurador de qualquiere Vniuerſidad
del Reyno ſea obligado a hazer parte,y a-
cuſarle criminalmente : y que a los tales ſe
les dè pena de açotes.

Figure 3.6   Law against the sale of fake saffron, a serious crime whose punishments included being whipped. *Source*: From *Prohibición contra los que hicieran o vendieran azafrán falso, promulgada en los Fueros de Aragón de 1564.*

fennel. Fresh and dried herbs included cilantro, mint, and vetiver, which is similar to lemongrass. Herbs were grown locally, and therefore were commonly used and very cheap to buy. The only spice that was grown in Iberia was saffron. However, it remained an incredibly expensive spice to purchase as collecting it was labor intensive. Spices were generally considered a luxury and one that was not suitable for the working classes. However, pepper was considered an exception.[92]

In the *Manual de mugeres*, there are multiple recipes that call for a variety of herbs and spices in both medicinal and cosmetic concoctions. Since these recipes were written for the wealthy in mind, there is no call for restraint on the amounts necessary for each recipe. The herbs that are most commonly used are lavender, rosemary, fennel, anise, parsley, and saffron. The uses range from aromatic pastes to mixtures to help with lactation. The spices that appear most often are cinnamon, ginger, nutmeg, and cloves. These spices can be found in recipes for a variety of uses: the bloody flux, tooth decay, face masks, and soaps.

In the *Calendario de Córdoba*, the month of June calls for the collection of medicinal plants including clover, absinth flowers, chamomile, and safflower.[93] The use of curative plants was common knowledge.[94] Fortified wine, often made with a number of spices, was used during the winter to protect those who were weak of chest or of spirit. In *Sevillana medicina*, one recipe for fortified wine calls for ginger, pepper, nutmeg, cinnamon, galangal, and cloves.[95]

HERBS AND SPICES IN LITERATURE

Spices are mentioned in the confection of electuaries, which were concoctions that combined medical and popular knowledge, and, in the texts of the Middle Ages, were often lauded for their almost magical properties. Using the Greek texts newly translated as the basis of their medicinal compounds, monks and nuns had at their disposal a number of recipes that called for sugar, honey, spices, and fruit. There were multiple ways in which people could buy these medicinal concoctions. One could buy electuaries from "authorized" sellers, including the aforementioned monks and nuns, and from apothecaries. Apothecaries, or medieval pharmacists, used a wide variety of spices to create medicinal compounds. Electuaries made with spices and sugar are mentioned more than once in *Libro de buen amor*. In this scene, Trotaconventos (the go-between, literally she who runs between convents) tells the archpriest that the nuns know how to treat their loved ones by providing them with electuaries to improve their sex drive:

Cominada alixandria, con el buen dia-gargante,
el diaçitron abatys, con el fino gengibrante,

miel rrosado, diaçiminio, diantioso va delante,
e la rroseta nouela que deuiera desir ante.

adraguea e elfenique con el estomatricon.
e la garriofilota con dia margariton,
tria sandaliz muy fyno con diasanturion,
que es, para doñear, preçiado e noble don.[96]

Candy with cumin seed from Alexandria, and gum

                                       tragacanth,

a monk's special recipe for citrus rind, with finest ginger,
honey of roses, cumin-seed sweets, sweets made of flowers,
and the new pink one, I should have mentioned before.

Sugar-coated sweets and almond paste, with cures for

                                       stomach-

ache, and elecutaries with gilly flower and those with

                                       powdered

pearls, very fine sandalwood mixed with *Satyrium trifolium*,
which is for lovemaking, a valued and noble gift.[97]

Pérez Vidal clarifies that the word *Satyrium*, which comes from the Greek word for ragwort, was known among the Greeks as well as the Arabs as an aphrodisiac.[98]

In medieval literature, the imagery of spices ranged from the practical to the metaphorical. The use of spices in Hebrew poetry hearkens back to the *Song of Songs*. In the eleventh-century poem "You Lie in my Palace," by Ibn Gabirol, spices are linked to sexual pleasure.

Ignore the mules and asses,
    And see to your guileless doe:
I'm here for one like you—and you for one like me.
    Who enters my chambers
finds my treasure: my pomegranate, my myrrh—
    my cinnamon, my nectar.[99]

Similar wording can be found in verse 8.2 of the *Song of Songs*:

I would lead you, I would bring you
To the house of my mother,
Of her who taught me—
I would let you drink of the spiced wine,
Of my pomegranate juice.[100]

Moshe ibn Ezra (1055 to after 1138) describes a perfect morning with the scent of spices in "Weak with Wine":

We woke, weak with wine from the party,
barely able to get up and walk
to the meadow wafting its spices—
    the scents of cassia and cloves:

and the sun had embroidered its surface with blossoms
    and across it spread a deep blue robe.[101]

Ibn Quzmān writes that it is sweet to sin during one's "salad days" or youth ("*es dulce pecar en días de lechuga e hinojo*"[102]), that is, days of "lettuce" and "fennel." Lettuce was known to cool one's ardor, whereas fennel was a known aphrodisiac.[103]

In literature, herbs and spices ranged from the practical to the metaphorical. In *Libro de buen amor*, spices appear as aphrodisiacs. In Hebrew and Arabic poetry, spices take on a more romantic mantle. The ostensible immorality of spices, as we will see, is related both to their exorbitant prices and their use in what would be considered foreign or non-Christian foods.

RELIGIOUS IMPLICATIONS

Both Christian health manuals and religious texts claimed that the consumption of meat could lead to lustful thoughts and deeds (carnality). A diet of vegetables and legumes cooled the body's urges. Lenten and monastic diets were heavily influenced by this notion. One of the criticisms of the Muslim and *morisco* population in the later Middle Ages was the accusation of hedonism. Remie Constable writes:

> By the later medieval and early modern period, Christian's perceptions of Muslim food and foodways had become laden with multiple and often conflicting meanings. On one hand, food from the Muslim world had long been perceived as luxurious, delicious, rich and sometimes rare (cultural delicacies, exotic spices). . . . On the other hand, Muslim food became associated with hedonism, epicureanism, love of luxury, gluttony and sinful behavior.[104]

Ironically, before the fifteenth century, Muslims were often criticized for eating a leguminous and vegetable-heavy diet.

Ideally, to eat in a Christian way was to eschew delicious foods for a sparer cuisine. In the *Corbacho*, Alfonso Martínez de Toledo warns his readers against the seven deadly sins. In the section titled "Gluttony," the author lists the foods that are consumed on a regular basis by those who are gluttonous.

Meat, fruit, and wine make the list, but neither vegetable nor legume is part of the "gluttony" list.[105]

Carolyn Walker Bynum tells us that abstinence in eating was practiced mainly as a way of "curing" bad behaviors.[106] Therefore women, seen as inherently sinful, would need to follow even stricter diets and were prone to extreme fasting. However, it must be noted that denying one's corporeality by eating sparingly or fasting was also a way in which women could subvert male authority and exert control over their own lives. In many depictions of female saints' lives, women survive on little. The hagiographical text of Saint Martha tells us, "*E en los primeros siete años non bivió saynón de vellotas e de landes e de rraizes e de yervas crudas e de frutas montesas*"[107] (and in the first seven years she lived only on acorns and roots, and raw herbs and wild fruits). Martha's holiness comes not only from her miraculous deeds but also from her lack of attention to her own needs.

Recalling the story of Saint Mary of Egypt, her wanton behavior lay in the cohabitation of gluttony and lust. In order for Mary to become a holy woman, she eschewed all trappings of a good life, but most especially good food: "*E despues que fueron comidos, bjuja delas yeruas asy commo las bestias*"[108] (And after [the breads] were eaten, she lived off of herbs like a wild beast). For the next thirty years, she lived off of the manna that angels brought to her. The text reads that during the first year of her penance, María was tempted many times by the devil, who brought her good things to eat.[109] The Christian audience would understand that the way to damnation was paved with delicious foods.

Since meat of any kind was forbidden during Lent, Christian eating became vegetarian or, at best, pescatarian during those forty days. As depicted by Lord Carnal's diet after his defeat at the hands of Lady Lent and her troops, Lent was not a time to be enjoying rich foods. Forty days of what could be considered an ascetic diet was not looked upon by many Christians with great joy. Cookbooks of the time maintained sections specifically for Lent like the section titled "*Tractado para guisar y aparejar las viandas del tiempo quaresmal*" (*Treatise on how to cook and prepare foods during Lent*) in Nola's *Libro de cozina*. Nola insists, however, that foods can be just as tasty during Lent as they are during the "meat times."[110] Of course, this section of the book is almost entirely made up of recipes for fish. For those people who did not have regular access to fresh fish, legumes, some vegetables, salted or preserved fish, and bread were to be the main staples of a Lenten diet.

Religious fasting, however, was not solely a Christian ritual. Both Muslim and Jewish traditions required religious fasting. However, the kinds of foods that they were allowed to eat were only restricted in so much as they were foods that they eschewed in general. With the exception of Passover, as the time of unleavened bread, most fasting rituals had more to do with atoning than rejecting certain foods.

The copious use of spice can be related to immorality and gluttony. As the Muslim diet became more suspicious in the fifteenth century for its supposed excess, "foreign" spices were also being questioned for their hedonistic character. King Ferdinand believed that there was nothing wrong with "good old domestic garlic."[111] Bernard of Clairvaux railed against spiced wines and fine dining, while Alain de Lille warned that too much fine dining (i.e., using spices and eating rich foods) could lead monks to homosexual temptations.[112] The difference between what moralists warned against and how the middle and upper classes ate, however, is vast.

At the close of the fifteenth century, eating certain legumes and vegetables was tantamount to a confession of Judaizing. As Gitlitz and Davidson tell us, certain vegetables, like chard and eggplant, and legumes, like chickpeas, were some of the most "charged" ingredients in Jewish kitchens.[113] The arrival of the Inquisition and the expulsion of the Jews from Iberia did much to create an atmosphere of intolerance and fear. This atmosphere bled into the domestic realm as servants began spying on their *converso* masters. However, it is too much to expect that centuries of food traditions could be changed overnight. As is indicated by the nostalgic list of food by Aldonza, it is clear that the influence of Muslim and Jewish traditions on the food culture of Iberia lessened as the country turned the corner into the sixteenth century but did not altogether disappear.

NOTES

1. Sancho Panza makes this observation to Don Quijote in chapter 2, part II.

2. Juan Gil, "Los Berenjeneros: The Aubergine Eaters," in *The Conversos and Moriscos in Late Medieval Spain and Beyond, vol 1: Departures and Change*, ed. Kevin Ingram (Leiden: Brill, 2009), 129.

3. Thomas Glick, *Islamic and Christian Spain in the Early Middle Ages* (Leiden: Brill, 2005), 77.

4. C. M. Woolgar, "Food and Taste in Europe in the Middle Ages," in *Food: The History of Taste,* ed. Paul Freedman (London: Thames & Hudson, 2007), 177.

5. Ibn Razīn al-Tugībī, *Relieves de las mesas, acerca de las delicias de la comida y los diferentes platos*, ed. and trans. Manuela Marín (Gijón, Spain: Ediciones Trea, S.L., 2007), 40.

6. Carolyn A. Nadeau, *Food Matters: Alonso Quijano's Diet and the Discourse of Early Modern Spain* (Toronto: University of Toronto Press, 2016), 132.

7. Massimo Montanari, *Medieval Tastes* (New York: Columbia University Press, 2018), 161.

8. James Anderson, *Daily Life during the Spanish Inquisition* (Westport, CT: Greenwood Press, 2002), 187.

9. Georges Duby, *Rural Economy and Country Life in the Medieval West*, trans. Cynthia Postan (Philadelphia: University of Pennsylvania Press, 1998), 273.

10. Expiración García Sánchez, "Los cultivos de Al-Andalus y su influencia en la alimentación." Aragón vive su historia: Actas de las II Jornadas Internacionales de Cultura Islámica. *Teruel: Instituto Occidental de Cultura Islámica* (1988): 183.

11. García Sánchez, *Los cultivos,* 188.

12. *Tesoro de la lengua castellana o española* (Madrid: Luis Sánchez, 1611), 479.

13. *Tesoro de la lengua castellana o española*, 669.

14. *Tesoro de la lengua castellana o española*, 498–99.

15. Real Academia Española, *Diccionario de la lengua Española* (Madrid: Real Academia Española 2001), www.rae.es/drae2001/hierba.

16. 'Abd al-Rahmān ibn Muhammad ibn Wāfid, *Tratado de agricultura*, trans. Cipriano Cuadrado Romero (Málaga: Analecta Malacitana, 1997), 87.

17. Ibn Wāfid, *Tratado de agricultura*, 86.

18. Ibn Wāfid, *Tratado de agricultura*, 101.

19. R. Dozy, ed., *Le Calendrier de Cordoue*, trans. Charles Pellat (Leiden: E.J. Brill, 1961), 48.

20. Dozy, *Le Calendrier,* 62.

21. Dozy, *Le Calendrier,* 76.

22. Dozy, *Le Calendrier,* 104.

23. Dozy, *Le Calendrier,* 118.

24. Dozy, *Le Calendrier,* 159.

25. Dozy, *Le Calendrier,* 172.

26. Teresa de Castro, *El abastecimiento alimentario en el Reino de Granada (1482–1510)* (Granada: Editorial Universidad de Granada, 2004), 348–49.

27. Tomás Puñal Fernández, *El Mercado en Madrid en la Baja Edad Media* (Madrid: Caja de Madrid, 1992), 234–35.

28. Glick, *Islamic and Christian Spain in the Early Middle Ages*, 78.

29. Olivia Remie Constable, "Food and Meaning: Christian Understandings of Muslim Food and Food Ways in Spain, 1250–1550," *Viator* 44, no. 3 (2013): 203.

30. 'Abū-Marwān 'Abd al-Malik ibn Abī al-'Alā' Ibn Zuhr, *Kitāb al-agdiya (Tratado de los alimentos)*, ed. Expiración García Sánchez (Madrid: Consejo Superior de Investigaciones Científicas, 1992), 95.

31. David M. Gitlitz and Linda Kay Davidson, *A Drizzle of Honey: The Lives and Recipes of Spain's Secret Jews* (New York: St. Martin's Press, 1999), 282.

32. Glick, *Islamic and Christian Spain in the Early Middle Ages*, 79.

33. Juan de Aviñon, *Sevillana Medicina* (Sevilla: Enrique Rasco, 1885), 69.

34. Ibn Wāfid, *Tratado de agricultura*, 87.

35. Aviñon, *Sevillana Medicina*, 69.

36. Aviñon, *Sevillana Medicina*, 70–71.

37. Aviñon, *Sevillana Medicina*, 94.

38. James Kritzeck, *Anthology of Islamic Literature: From the Rise of Islam to Modern Times* (New York: Holt, Rinehart, and Winston, 1964), 145.

39. Aviñon, *Sevillana Medicina*, 95–96.

40. Moses Maimonides, *Medical Aphorisms Treatises 1–5*, trans. Gerrit Bos (Salt Lake City: Brigham Young University Press, 2004), 91–93.

41. Aviñon, *Sevillana Medicina*, 97.

42. Aviñon, *Sevillana Medicina*, 97.

43. Maimonides, *Medical Aphorisms*, 93.

44. Aviñon, *Sevillana Medicina*, 98–99.

45. Aviñon, *Sevillana Medicina*, 100.

46. Al-Tugībī, *Relieves de las mesas*, 36–37.

47. Al-Tugībī, *Relieves de las mesas*, 263.

48. Al-Tugībī, *Relieves de las mesas*, 264–66.

49. Al-Tugībī, *Relieves de las mesas*, 268–77.

50. Marín (in Al-Tugībī, *Relieves de las mesas*, 268n274) cites a French travelogue from the sixteenth century that confirms that, at least in Egypt, the inhabitants ate eggplant in the most amazing array of dishes.

51. See chapter 1.

52. Joan Santanach, ed., *The Book of Sent Soví: Medieval Recipes from Catalonia*, trans. Robin Vogelzang (Barcelona: Barcino-Tamesis, 2014), 115.

53. Gitlitz and Davidson, *A Drizzle of Honey*, 77–78.

54. Gitlitz and Davidson, *A Drizzle of Honey*, 77–78.

55. Quoted in Gitlitz and Davidson, *A Drizzle of Honey*, 46.

56. Ruberto de Nola, *Libro de cozina* (Barcelona: Paneuropea de Ediciones y Publicaciones, 1972), 144.

57. Gitlitz and Davidson, *A Drizzle of Honey*, 61.

58. Gitlitz and Davidson, *A Drizzle of Honey*, 155.

59. Gitlitz and Davidson, *A Drizzle of Honey*, 157–58.

60. Al-Tugībī, *Relieves de las mesas*, 33.

61. Quoted in Nadeau, *Food Matters*, 152.

62. Juan Ruiz, *The Book of Good Love*, trans. Elizabeth Drayson MacDonald, ed. Melveena McKendrick (London: Everyman, 1999), 268, st. 1067.

63. Ruiz, *The Book of Good Love*, 269, st. 1067.

64. Ruiz, *The Book of Good Love*, 276, st. 1102.

65. Ruiz, *The Book of Good Love*, 277, st. 1102.

66. Aviñon, *Sevillana Medicina*, 94.

67. Arnaldo de Vilanova, *Régimen de Salud*, ed. Juan Cruz Cruz (Huesca, Spain: La Val de Onsera, 1997), 118.

68. Barbara E. Kurtz, "'De la obra de la tienda de don Amor': Facetas de la alegoría del *Libro de buen amor*," *Romance Quarterly* 33, no. 2 (1986): 182.

69. Ruiz, *The Book of Good Love*, 316, st. 1280.

70. Ruiz, *The Book of Good Love*, 319, l. 1286c.

71. Ruiz, *The Book of Good Love*, 318, ll. 1288ab.

72. Ruiz, *The Book of Good Love*, 318, l. 1289c.

73. Ruiz, *The Book of Good Love*, 320, st. 1290.

74. Ruiz, *The Book of Good Love* 320, st. 1297.

75. Kurtz, "'De la obra de la tienda,'" 185.

76. María Jesús Rubiera Mata, "La dieta de Ibn Quzmān: Notas sobre la alimentación andalusí a través de su literatura," in *La alimentación en las culturas islámicas*, edited by Manuela Marín and David Waines (Madrid: Agencia Española de Cooperación Internacional, 1994), 130.

77. Ibn Quzmān, *Cancionero andalusí*, ed. Federico Corriente (Madrid: Ediciones Hiperión, 1996), 95.

78. Ibn Quzmān, *Cancionero andalusí*, 320.

79. Henri Pérès, *Esplendor de al-Andalus*, trans. Mercedes García-Arenal (Madrid: Hiperión, 1953), 199.

80. Pérès, *Esplendor de al-Andalus*, 199.

81. Pérès, *Esplendor de al-Andalus*, 200.

82. Quoted in Olivia Remie Constable, "Food and Meaning," 217–18.

83. Luis de Usoz y Río, *Cancionero de obras de burlas provocantes a risa* (Madrid, 1841), 88–89.

84. Paul Freedman, *Out of the East* (New Haven: Yale University Press, 2008), 26.

85. Freedman, *Out of the East*, 128.

86. Freedman, *Out of the East*, 128.

87. Freedman, *Out of the East*, 126.

88. Expiración García Sánchez, "Especias y condimentos en la sociedad andalusí: Prácticas culinarias y aplicaciones dietéticas," in *El sabor del sabor: Hierbas aromáticas, condimentos y especias*, ed. Antonio Garrido Arando (Córdoba: Universidad de Córdoba, 2004), 91.

89. Freedman, *Out of the East*, 56.

90. Gitlitz and Davidson, *A Drizzle of Honey*, 36.

91. Freedman, *Out of the East*, 24.

92. Freedman, *Out of the East*, 43.

93. Dozy, *Le Calendrier*, 104.

94. José Pérez Vidal, *Medicina y dulcería en el Libro de buen amor* (Madrid: Cupsa Editorial, 1981), 29.

95. Aviñón, *Sevillana Medicina*, 153–54.

96. Ruiz, *The Book of Good Love*, 330, stanzas 1335–6.

97. Ruiz, *The Book of Good Love*, 331, stanzas 1335–6.

98. Pérez Vidal, *Medicina y dulcería*, 223.

99. Peter Cole, ed. and trans., *The Dream of the Poem: Hebrew Poetry from Muslim and Christian Spain 950–1492* (Princeton: Princeton University Press, 2007), 99.

100. *Sefaria: A Living Library of Jewish Texts*, accessed November 9, 2020, www.sefaria.org/texts, 8.2.

101. Cole, *The Dream of the Poem*, 122.

102. Ibn Quzmān, *Cancionero andalusí*, 199, st. 71, l. 3b.

103. Rubiera Mata, "La dieta de Ibn Quzmān," 135.

104. Remie Constable, "Food and Meaning," 202.

105. Alfonso Mártinez de Toledo, *Arcipreste de Talavera o Corbacho,* ed. Michael Gerli (Madrid: Cátedra, 1998) 130–31.

106. Caroline Walker Bynum, *Holy Feast and Holy Fast* (Berkeley: University of California Press, 1987), 199.

107. John K. Moore Jr., *Libro de los huéspedes (Escorial MS h.I.13): A Critical Edition* (Tempe: Arizona Center for Medieval and Renaissance Studies, 2008), 16, ll. 126–28.

108. Moore, *Libro de los huéspedes*, 31, ll. 193–94.

109. Moore, *Libro de los huéspedes*, 31.

110. de Nola, *Libro de cozina*, 117.

111. Jack Turner, *Spice* (New York: Knopf, 2004), 285.

112. Freedman, *Out of the East*, 151–52.

113. Gitlitz and Davidson, *A Drizzle of Honey*, 36.

Chapter 4

Fruits and Sweets

The revolutionary changes in the technology of watering allowed orchards and vineyards to thrive in the Middle Ages. A wide variety of fruits became part of the daily fare of those who either grew them or had the money to purchase fruit in the marketplace. Commonly grown fruits were figs, apples, pears, cherries, peaches, and plums. Figs became one of the most sought-after fruits, having been introduced to the Iberian Peninsula by the Muslims. Glick writes that Malagan figs were exported by Muslim and Christian traders and sold in Baghdad, India, and China.[1] Like vegetables and legumes, fruit held a particular place of importance in the diets of the Middle Ages. Some fruits were considered a staple food while others were considered more of a delicacy.

Fruits were consumed in a number of different forms: compotes, jams, dried, or as a component of a dessert. According to James Anderson, refreshing drinks were made with a variety of fruit juices and snow, transported from the mountains and deposited in snow pits in the city.[2] Like vegetables, fruits were sold both in the marketplace and by roving fruit sellers. The prices, however, were fixed, and there were heavy fines for those who bought fruit directly from the grower and resold them in the city.[3]

The *Calendario de Córdoba* details the planting and harvesting of fruits and sugar cane throughout the year as well as the best times to make preserves and syrup. In January, sugar cane is harvested, preserves of cider and carrots are put up, along with lemon syrup.[4] In February, pear and apple trees are to be transplanted.[5] March sees the planting of sugarcane along with the flowering of the fruit trees.[6] April is a busy month, filled with the preparations of rose oil, syrups, and flower waters. It is also the month to stake lemon trees and plant melons.[7] May holds the first real bounty of early fruits. Olives and grapes begin to grow; bees are making their honey;

apples, pears, apricots and cherries begin to appear.[8] May is also the time
to make preserves of nuts, and apple syrup.[9] In June, coastal figs begin to
appear, as do blackberries.[10] In July grapes ripen, pistachios grow, sweet and
sour pears are ready to be picked.[11] In August, one should make pomegranate juice with two kinds of pomegranates. The author also mentions that the
mixture of this juice with fennel makes an excellent eyewash for all kinds
of eye ailments. Asian dates are beginning to mature, and peaches, late
sweet pears, and watermelon are ready to pick.[12] In September, along with a
number of fruits that are ready to pick (dates, pomegranates, and peaches),
both bananas and sugar cane are beginning to grow.[13] October brings the
beginning of the olive harvest and the making of quince syrup or cordial.[14]
In November acorns and chestnuts are harvested, and the bayberry (from the
myrtle bush) is made into a medicinal syrup. The rest of the bounty is vegetables and legumes. In preparation for a cold winter, fruit trees are covered
in November, and little is seen to grow until the year begins again with the
harvest of sugar cane.[15]

In chapter 13 of the medical treatise *Sevillana Medicina,* Juan de Aviñon
gives the reader an exhaustive list of the merits and demerits of the fruits
available for consumption. Like the variety of vegetables, fruits too were
plentiful and a good source of calories. The fruits Aviñon mentions are both
dried and fresh, and include figs, grapes, plums, a variety of berries, cherries,
pears, peaches, apples, pomegranates, quince, and a number of citrus fruits.
Nuts, also technically dried fruits or fruit seeds, are mentioned in this chapter
and include almonds, walnuts, hazelnuts, pistachios, and pine nuts.

Using Galen as one of his authoritative sources, he lauds figs and grapes
as the two most healthful fruits: *"Dize Galieno que las uvas y los figos son
las mejores de todas las fructas"* (Galen says that grapes and figs are the best
of all the fruits).[16] Accordingly, figs are full of nutrients, engender healthy
blood, calm coughs, and help with kidney function. Although most fruits
humorally are cold and wet or cold and dry, figs and grapes are warm and
wet. Dried figs and raisins are also mentioned as good for one's health and
appear in many recipes of all three religions. *"Pasas—calientes y húmedas—
amigas del fígado y conviértense en buena sangre y en buen humor, y sueltan
la cámara, y abren las opilaciones de los pechos y amansan la tosse"* (Raisins, warm and damp, are healthy for the liver and engender healthy blood,
loosen the bowels, and calm coughs).[17]

Fruit juices are especially healthful, according to Aviñon. Grape juice
helps stomach ailments. Apple and pear juice are useful for building up one's
strength.[18] He also mentions that of all the fruits, pears and apples are the
slowest to rot.[19] Pomegranates and quince are very healthy; pomegranates
soothe hunger as well as anger, and both of these *"esfuerçen el estómago"*
(strengthen the stomach).[20]

Arab physicians saw fruits as more useful in their pharmacological mixtures than as consumable fresh fruit. García Sánchez writes, "*Se consumían las frutas solas, frescas o pasas, en formas de zumos o en compotas y mermeladas, y con las uvas—mosto, arrope(zumo de uvas) nabīd (bebida alcohólica) y vino*" (They consumed fresh and dried fruit in forms of juice, compotes, jams, and in drinks like grape juice, alcohol, and wine).[21] Aviñon does mention that a number of fruits can produce melancholy, fevers, or bad blood, especially cherries and blackberries.[22] However, all of these medical opinions are based on the varieties of a particular fruit, in what state of maturity they are, and how they are eaten.

Maimonides enumerates both good and bad qualities of fruits and their uses in medicinal concoctions. About apples he writes:

> The smell of an apple strengthens the heart and the brain and is beneficial for those suffering from marasmus and delusions. However, as to its [actual] consumption, he states that it is more harmful than the consumption of any other fruit because its fragrance gives rise to gases in the nerves and in the muscles that can only be dissolved with difficulty.

And pears:

> Pears strengthen the stomach and have the special property of quenching thirst when eaten after a meal. If one lets their juice stand, it turns into a vinegar that strengthens the stomach in a wonderful way and does not harm the nerves because of the astringency and fragrance that it contains.[23]

Nuts fare very well for both satisfying hunger and for nutritional value. Aviñon mentions specifically that almond milk is good for those who are ill. Almond milk is used frequently in both sweet and savory dishes. Of the other nuts commonly available, hazelnuts and pistachios seem, in his opinion, to be the most nutritious and, in the case of pistachios, give one a sexual appetite (*ayudan a dar apetito a dormir con muger*). The other nuts, however, are also found to be favorable to one's health. Their benefits include easing a cough, aiding in digestion, and helping with kidney issues.[24]

Maimonides warns that excessive consumption of walnuts causes stuttering, but pistachios are the most healthful of fruits.

> They strengthen the stomach and the liver by their special property. Their oil has the same effect if rubbed on the stomach and liver. They are beneficial in many ways. If they are eaten either alone or with raisins and sugar before the meal, during the meal, or after the meal, they are beneficial for all conditions. They are of moderate heat and dryness.[25]

Vilanova writes that nuts that are "oleaginous," meaning that oil can be produced from them, and are harmful if eaten raw. These would include almonds, walnuts, and pine nuts. However, he believed that if they are mixed with sugar or honey, they are delicious and healthful.[26] Pistachios and hazelnuts, both warm and dry in humoral makeup, provide more nutrition than other nuts because of their humoral qualities.[27] Most nuts were affordable to all economic classes and therefore provided a much-needed source of protein.[28]

Honey was the most accessible sweetener in the Middle Ages. Many people were able to keep bees to produce their own honey (see figure 4.1). One of the longest chapters in the *Tratado de agricultura* is devoted to apiculture. The text outlines how to choose the queens, how to kill parasites, how to move the hives, how to cure ailing hives, and tricks to avoid being attacked by the bees.[29]

In the tenth and eleventh centuries, sugar was an expensive import, coming from the Middle East. In the twelfth and thirteenth centuries, however, sugar began to be cultivated in small amounts in and around Andalucía and in the

Figure 4.1   Bees/honey. *Source:* From the abridged Latinized MS Rome 4182 housed in the Biblioteca Casanatense in Rome, 1390–1400 (Cat. MS 4182).

area around Valencia. According to the *Calendario de Córdoba*, sugar cane was planted in March and harvested in January. January and February were considered the "sugar months."[30]

It wasn't until the fifteenth century that sugar was produced in larger quantities in Iberia.[31] The word *azúcar* comes from the Arabic word *sukkar* (which comes from the Persian *sakar*).[32] Fábregas García writes that sugar produced in Andalucía was sold throughout the Western world. She also points out that varying qualities of sugar were being produced, which allowed for people of differing economic statuses to afford some sugar in their diets.[33] García Sánchez claims, however, that sugar was still hard to come by for most people and that honey was the sweetener of choice throughout the Middle Ages.[34]

Honey was the preferred sweetener for pharmacological mixtures, although sugar started creeping its way into medicines as early as the tenth century.[35] A number of Muslim physicians discuss the benefits of sugar for medicinal purposes. In Ibn al-Bāytar's book titled *Sugar in the Comprehensive Book of Simple Drugs* he summarizes the use of sugar in multiple medical sources throughout the centuries. Among the medical men he cites are Dioscorides, Galen, and al-Razi, all of whom we have seen discussed in a number of Christian medical treatises as well. He also cites Ibn al-Nafis, known as the second Ibn Sina (Damascus, d. 1288).[36] There seems to have been a consensus that a paste made with white sugar was useful for ailments of the eyes like trachoma. Since sugar was considered hot and dry, humorally speaking, it was used to balance the humors of those who found themselves cold and wet. Sugar was also used for stomach ailments and sore throats.[37]

Most recipes called for white sugar, although some physicians believed that red sugar, or raw sugar, was considered gentler on the body. Creating and selling electuaries, medicinal concoctions mentioned in chapter 3 (see section on Spices), became a booming business in the Middle Ages. Sugar and honey were recommended for melancholy or ill temper and were considered helpful for liver function.[38] Indeed, the saying "a spoonful of sugar makes the medicine go down" would not have been lost on most physicians of the Middle Ages.

As sugar became more common, it was often added to electuaries. Trotaconventos tells the archpriest that the nuns were experts at making these sugary confections:

Sabed que de todo açucar ally anda bolando,
poluo, terron e candy e mucho del rrosado
açucar de confites e açucar violado,
E de muchas otras guisas que yo he oluidado.[39]

I tell you, all kinds of sugar brim over there,
powdered or in lumps or candy or rose sugar,
confectionery sugar and violet sugar,
and lots of other kinds I have forgotten.[40]

Carles Vela writes that by the fifteenth century, the dispensing of medicines became increasingly important; apothecaries were creating a "virtual monopoly over the production of sugared comfits" as well as sophisticated remedies for a variety of complaints.[41]

The *Manual de mugeres* uses sugar in many medicinal mixtures. For example, a recipe for a cough calls for very fine sugar, a mash of beans, licorice root, oregano, and fennel.[42] Another concoction for a face mask called for a half pound of black figs, a quarter pound of good raisins, a small amount of sesame seeds, mashed together with honey and egg white.[43] In home remedies, the line between medical and culinary mixtures was hazy at best.

The combination of sweet and savory is common in recipes of all three religions. Both fresh and dried fruits are used in a number of recipes for meat dishes. The *Book of Sent Soví* calls for raisins in a recipe for "Stuffed mutton shoulder."[44] Sugar, cinnamon, and cloves are used in a recipe for "Bird Turnovers."[45] In *A Drizzle of Honey,* dried figs and dried apricots take a primary place in a chicken recipe, and apples and almonds are served with roast goose.[46] In *Relieves de las mesas*, many recipes combine sweet and savory, including recipes for beef with prunes, honey, or a compote made of honeyed roses.[47] Lamb can be cooked with apples or quince.[48] A large number of the meat recipes are also cooked with almonds, pine nuts, chestnuts, and acorns.[49]

Sugar swept the nation as an expensive and exotic treat. Nadeau writes, "Sugar's role in later Spanish cookbooks is significant—in the *Sent Soví,* sugar appears in a third of the recipes and in Nola—even more."[50] In the *Sent Soví,* a recipe for fritters calls for leavened wheat dough mixed with eggs. To fry the fritters, the recipe calls for "good, clean pork grease" and a "good pan that is nice and clean." After frying the fritters, "put them on a nice plate, and put plenty of sugar over and under them." These would be served, according to the book, at the end of the meal instead of cheese.[51] In Nola's *Libro de cozina* a recipe for fruit turnovers calls for toasted almonds and hazelnuts to be mixed in with the wheat dough. The turnovers are to be filled with a mixture of honey and dried fruit and basted with sugar and water before baking them.[52]

Since *Manual de mugeres* was a book that was written with the elite in mind, liberal amounts of sugar are called for in recipes as well as in the medicinal compounds. Recipes include marzipan, cakes, doughnuts, and puff pastries. One recipe for sponge cake calls for two pounds of sugar, white wine, anis, and white flour.[53] The puff pastries call for almond milk, sugar, and lard. The doughnuts also call for almond milk and ground almonds. After frying the doughnuts in "good oil," the recipe calls for a coating of honey, sugar, cinnamon, and toasted pine nuts.[54] "Good oil" was most likely heated lard rather than olive oil since Christians tended to fry in lard.

Arab cooking manuals of medieval Iberia show a marked inclination toward sweets.[55] Gitlitz and Davidson point out that the thirteenth-century *Baghdad Cookery-Book*'s entire ninth chapter is devoted to *halva*. Other sweets made with ground nuts and sugar are *alfajores* and marzipan.[56] *Halva*, or *halwā* is mentioned in a number of sources, including *Hisba* manuals. This sweet, made of sesame seed paste, is one of the precursors of the more common Spanish sweet, *turrón*. García Sánchez writes that the first recipe for *turrón* can be found in Enrique de Villena's *Arte cisoria* in 1421.[57]

Chapter 4 of *Relieves* is devoted to the variety of *roscas* and *buñuelos* that were typically eaten. *Roscas* are round pastries made with bread flour and often filled with nuts and sugar. *Buñuelos* are the typical fried fritters for which the Muslims in Spain were famous. These were usually dipped in sugar and cinnamon or honey. Section 9 of *Relieves*, which consists of seven chapters, covers all manner of sweet confections, from the simplest recipes called *fanid* (hard crack candy made of boiled sugar) to *halva*. Sweets like nougat and hard sesame candies also make an appearance in the cookbook. Marín points out that Ibn Razīn uses honey in as many recipes as he does sugar, which demonstrates the ubiquity of that sweetener.[58] Other sweeteners that appear in the cookbook are syrups made of sugar and other flavorings, especially rose water.

Gitlitz and Davidson write that the desserts of the Iberian Jews were identical to those of their "Christian neighbors."[59] Pastes made of quince, sugar candies, and holiday *turrón* along with all sorts of fried pastries can be found among the recipes of *A Drizzle of Honey*. The one exception, Passover fritters, are made with crushed *matzo* rather than flour.[60]

FRUITS AND SWEETS IN LITERATURE

Like grains and meat, fruit maintains a dual nature in the Christian literature of the Middle Ages; fruit can be seen as both holy and sinful. Stephen Nichols writes:

> Because the foundational myths of Christian society linked the social ritual of eating to the Fall and its redemption, the medieval food metaphor always contained the seeds of parable and was ever ready to stress the dynamics of narrative exemplarity. To eat was not to replenish, so much as to reenact historical loss and the promise of salvation from that loss.[61]

The introduction of Berceo's *Milagros* is replete with food metaphors. The narrative within the introduction tells of man's encounter with the Virgin's good works as they are presented in Scripture, in the writings of the church fathers, and also as they are made manifest in nature. This encounter completes the circle of life and allows for man to be restored to grace.

The text depicts a Christian paradise awaiting all those who seek forgiveness. Berceo begins his description of paradise on Earth by describing the kinds of trees that can be found there:

Avién y grand abondo   de buenas arboledas,
milgranos e figueras,   peros e mazanedas,
e muchas otras fructas   e diversas monedas,
mas non avié ningunas   podridas [nin] azedas.[62]

There was a profusion of fine trees—
pomegranate and fig, pear and apple,
and many other fruits of various kinds.
But none were spoiled or sour.[63]

In this postlapsarian paradise, no birds sing off key and no fruit is rotten. Berceo reminds us, however, that fruit was also the cause of the fall, and therefore can lead one to grave temptations:

El fructo de los árbores   era dulz e sabrido,
si don Adám oviesse   de tal fructo comido,
de tan mala manera   non serié decibido,
ni tomarién tal danno   Eva [nin] so marido.[64]

The fruit of the trees was sweet and delicious;
if Adam had eaten such fruit,
he would not have been so badly deceived.
Neither Eve nor her husband would have suffered such harm![65]

Berceo uses his introduction as a conduit between the Old Testament and the New Testament. He warns the reader to beware of temptation, but he continues with the fruit metaphors to describe the Virgin herself:

Es dicha vid, es uva,   almendra, malgranada,
que de granos de graçia   está toda calcada,
oliva, cedro, bálssamo,   palma bien ajumada,
piértega en que sovo   la serpiente alzada.[66]

She is called Vine, she is Grape, Almond, and Pomegranate,
replete with its grains of grace,
Olive, Cedar, Balsam, leafy Palm,
Rod upon which the serpent was raised.[67]

Pomegranates maintain a religious significance in both Judaism and Christianity. They are often consumed during Rosh Hashanah and are said to have exactly 613 seeds, which correspond to the 613 *mitzvot* (religious commandments) found in the Torah.[68] Medieval and Early Modern paintings often depict the Virgin Mary and the baby Jesus with a pomegranate (see figure 4.2). There are multiple theories about the meaning of the pomegranate in Christianity: the unity of the Church, fertility, resurrection, or the fullness of Christ's suffering.[69] The almond is a symbol of divine favor and the purity of Mary.[70] The grape, and by association the vine, represent Holy Communion.

Electuaries make an appearance in the *Milagros* but in a very different context than the one found in *Libro de buen amor*. These elecutaries were used as remedies for moral ills.

In miracle 7, "San Pedro y el monje mal ordenado" (St. Peter and the Proud Monk), Berceo writes:

Figure 4.2 *Madonna and Child with a Pomegranate*, by Lorenzo di Credi, 1475/1480.
Source: Samuel H. Kress Collection (open access).

Por salud de su cuerpo   e por vevir más sano,
usava lectüarios   apriesa e cutiano,
en ivierno calientes,   e fríos en verano,
devrié andar devotoe   andava lozano.[71]

For his body's sake and to live more soundly,
He used electuaries every day:
In winter, warm ones, and in summer, cold.
He should have been devout, but he was lustful.[72]

The electuaries in this text are made with honey, which was used to control one's libido.[73] Bees make an appearance in miracle 12, "*El prior de San Salvador y el sacristan Uberto*" ("The Prior and Uberto the Sexton"). In this tale, the Virgin Mary takes pity on a prior who suffers in purgatory for his filthy mouth:

¡Grado a la Gloriosa   que es de gracia plena!
fuera só del lazerio,   essido só de pena;
caí em dulz vergel   cerca de dulz colmena,
do nunqua veré mengua   de yantar nin de cena.[74]

Thanks be to the Glorious One who is full of grace!
I am free from misery; I have come out of suffering;
I fell into a sweet garden near a sweet beehive,
where I will see no lack of dinner or supper.[75]

Both the garden and the beehives allude to the introduction of the collection. The garden is paradise on earth, and the bee, according to Mount and Grant Cash, "symbolizes virginity since bees were thought to reproduce asexually, or by parthenogenesis," like the Virgin herself.[76]

Fruit in *Libro de buen amor* is used either as an enticement or to represent sexual pleasure. In one scene, Don Melón applies to Trotaconventos for help wooing his love Endrina. The go-between's aid involves offering Endrina tasty treats:

Nunca esta mi tyenda syn fruta a las loçanas,
muchas pera e durasnos, ¡que çidras e que mancanas!
¡que castanas, que piñones e que muchas avellanas!
las que vos queredes mucho estas vos seran mas sanas.[77]

My shop always has plenty of fruit for beautiful girls,
lots of pears and peaches, such citrons and apples!
Wonderful chestnuts, pine kernels, no end of hazelnuts!

The ones you like the best will do you the most good.[78]

Endrina agrees to accompany Trotaconventos "*a tomar de la su fruta e a la pella jugar*"[79] ("To try her fruit and play ball games"[80]). The fruit that she will try is, of course, Don Melón. This scene can be read parodically and medicinally. Don Melón, true to his name, is both egotistical (big headed) and sexual (rich and juicy). The definition of *Endrina* is sloe berry; bitter and in need of both heat and moisture to make her palatable. Indeed, the wet melon will do wonders for the dry sloe berry. The audience of the time would have understood the references, both humoral and humoristic.

Lord Love's aforementioned ekphrastic tent (see chapter 3) reflects the agricultural calendars of the Middle Ages. In the summertime, the harvesting of fruit takes a central role. The rich men who represent summertime "ripen fruit," "lunch on rhubarb," and eat "early figs."[81] Stanza 1291 reads:

Enxeria los arbores con ajena cortesa,
comia nueuos palales, sudaua syn peresa,
boluia las aguas frias de su naturalesa,
traya las manos tyntas de la mucha çeresa.[82]

He grafted the trees with new bark,
ate new honeycomb, sweated freely.
He drank the cold water of fountains and springs.
His hands were stained red with cherry juice.[83]

Honey, figs, and cherries are part of the bounty of the Spanish summer. The cherries and their juice may also be read as sexual humor. Cherries—ripe, plump, and juicy—were ready to be picked and enjoyed.

Both Muslim and Jewish poetical traditions demonstrate a great fondness for fruits. Ibn Quzmān mentions a variety of fruits in his poetry including pomegranates (his favorite), peaches, apples, and grapes. Dried fruits and nuts are also mentioned, but Rubiera Mata clarifies that these were "luxury products" that were offered during holidays.[84]

Rather than sexual satire, as we see in *Libro de buen amor*, Ibn Quzmān uses fruit as erotic metaphor. In *zéjel* 10, verse 6 Quzmān writes:

De poma son tus pechitos;
de adárgama, las mejillas;
de aljófar, los dientecillos,
y de azúcar, la boquita.[85]

And breasts like apples,

cheeks like flour,
teeth like pearls,
and a mouth of sugar.

Zéjel 100 verse 2 reads:

Su boca exhala almizcle fragante,
en ella Dios colocóle aljófar
jurarías que es de azúcar
allí molido, y licor en vaso:
quien la besa, halla la vida.[86]

From her mouth a fragrant musk,
in it God has placed a pearl
you would swear it was made of fine sugar, and bottled liquor:
Whoever kisses her has found life.

In *zéjel* 17 verse 5, Ibn Quzmān compares the mention of his love as sweeter than a pastry:

¿Ves qué dulce es a la lengua tu mención?
Es más dulce para el alma que el pastel.[87]

Do you see how sweet your name is on my tongue?
It is sweeter to my soul than a pastry.

Pastries in the form of ladyfingers, are compared, quite aptly, to the fingers of his love in *zéjel* 1, verse 5:

Rubito, dulce, hermoso, delgado y alto
con dedos de noble, cortesano y pendolista,
que parecen los de quien amasa mazapán,
tanto, que al verlos se asombrara un pastelero.[88]

Tall, sweet, handsome, thin, and tall
with the noble fingers of a courtier or calligrapher,
that seem like those that would produce marzipan,
so much that they would astonish a pastry chef.

Fruit appears almost exclusively in ibn Quzmān's poetry as metaphor. Fruit consumption, as depicted in his poetry, is generally in the form of wine.

The Hebrew poet Moshe ibn Ezra spent much of his early life living in comfort in Granada. In the wake of the Almoravid invasion of 1090, however, his family, writes Peter Cole, had their fortune confiscated and the poet eventually had to leave Granada. He spent his remaining years wandering in the Christian north, "bemoaning the loss of his Andalusian world and its glories."[89] It is not surprising then, that his poems can be both nostalgic and bitter. In the poem "The Gazelle's Sigh" the poet uses cakes and fruit to remind the reader of the sweetness of youth, which implies a nostalgia for the time of more tolerance:

Hurry to homes of beloveds whom Time
    has scattered and left behind in ruins;
what once were the dwellings of graceful does
    are lairs now to lions and wolves.
I hear the gazelle's sigh and her wailing
    from Edom's prison, and Arabia's jail;
she weeps for the bridegroom of her youth
    and calls in pleasing song to Him:
"Sustain me with cakes of nuts and raisins;
    revive me with apples of your love."[90]

Both the apple tree and the fruit itself appear with some regularity in Hebrew poetry of the Middle Ages. The source of the image of the apple comes from the Song of Songs:

Like an apple tree among the trees of the forest,
So is my beloved among the youths.
I delight to sit in his shade,
And his fruit is sweet to my mouth.[91]

The shade and fragrance of the apple tree represents God's love. The fruit of the tree, its lushness and sweetness, represent earthly delights. Yehuda HaLevi, a contemporary of Moshe ibn Ezra and, Cole writes, "an unrivaled master of Hebrew and its prosody,"[92] emphasizes the uniqueness of his love by referring to the superiority of the apple in his poem titled "Another Apple":

You bound me, doe of delight, in your beauty
    and in that captivity worked me ruthlessly.
Since parting came between us that day,
    nothing I've seen has matched your grace.
And so, I turn to an apple for succor
    whose fragrance recalls your breath like myrrh—
its shape, your breast, and its color the flush
    that races through your cheeks when you blush.[93]

Fruit can represent both the beauty of God and nature, and the deception of sweetness. Sweets can also be intoxicating and shallow. The taste of them is pleasurable but leaves us wanting more. Scheindlin's translation of Ibn Ezra's poem of lost love and regret demonstrates the negative aspect of sweets:

Charming even in deceit;
The fruit of his mouth is like candy sweet.
Played me false, that little cheat![94]

Fruits are easily associated with love and lust because of their inherent lushness and sweetness. And, logically, unripe fruit provokes sadness and bitterness. However, as we see in Berceo's poems, fruits are also heavenly. Associated with the goodness of the Virgin Mary and the perfection of Heaven as the postlapsarian garden, the bounty of the earth gives way to the bounty of paradise. Sweets, pastries, sugar, and honey play an important role in the metaphoric nature of the Arabic and Hebrew poetical traditions. Sugar and honey can be both tempting, addicting, and treacherous.

The use of fruits and sweets in the literature of the Middle Ages gives the reader insight into the regard with which the people of the time held them both. Because our modern diet is filled with sugar and sweets, it is difficult to comprehend that sweets were not a part of everyday life in the Middle Ages. Many would have only tasted sweets and dried fruits during holidays. And the ubiquity of sugar was still many years away.

RELIGIOUS IMPLICATIONS

Stephen Nichols quotes one of the sermons of Saint Bernard of Clairvaux who comments on the slippery slope of self-indulgence:

Inattentiveness to the self first overtakes sinners; then curiosity about material things that do not concern them; then desire for these things; covetousness counsels yielding to temptation; the first experience becomes habit; habit becomes open scorn for the law; and scorn soon translates to evil which consists in open attachment to and enjoyment of a sin.[95]

Pleasure in all forms could come at a moral cost to Christians in the Middle Ages. Seeking pleasure often led to an excess of all desires. Moderation required a tempered diet. Consuming fruits and sweets, then, could lead one to excesses of other types of pleasure: a sinner could be gluttonous in more than one fashion. In the litany of sins illustrated in *Libro de buen amor,* the archpriest introduces the sin of gluttony in stanza 294:

Adan, el nuestro padre, por gula e tragonia,
por que comio del fruto que comer non deuia,
echole del parayso dios en aquesse dia;
por ello en el infierno desque morio yazia.[96]

Adam our father, in greed and gluttony,
ate the fruit forbidden to him,
and God threw him out of paradise at once.
When he died he went to Hell for it.[97]

He also blames gluttony for the sins of Lot:

ffeciste por la gula a lot, noble burges,
beuer tanto que yugo con sus fijas, pues ves
a fazer tu forniçio; Ca do mucho vino es,
luego es la logxuria E todo mal despues.[98]

Through gluttony you made Lot, that noble townsman,
Drink so much that he lay with his daughters
And fornicated, for where a lot of wine is drunk,
Lust creeps in, and all other evils with it.[99]

    Christian moralists of the time saw gluttony and lust as inevitably linked. The fifteenth-century poet Alfonso Martínez de Toledo devotes an entire chapter of his moralizing text, *Corbacho,* to the perils of sweets and fruits. Francesc Eiximenis condemned fried fritters, and Hernando de Talavera, Queen Isabel's confessor, lambasted the Muslims for their habit of eating dried fruit.

    Martínez de Toledo condemns the consumption of all fruits in the chapter on the sin of gluttony:

Frutas, de diversas guisas, vengan do quiera, cuesten lo que costaren. En la primavera barrines, guindas, ceruelas, alvérchigas, figos, bevras, duraznos, melones, peras vinosas e de la Vera, mançanas, xabíes, romíes, granadas dulçes e agradulçes e azedas, figo doñengal e uva moscatel.[100]

Various kinds of fruit, from wherever they may originate, at whatever cost. In spring apricots, cherries, plums, soft peaches, figs, early figs, hard peaches, melons, winey pears and those from la Vera, wild apples, cultivated apples, sweet bittersweet and sour pomegranates, red figs, and muscatel grapes.

He continues by enumerating a number of sweets that open the appetite to excessive overeating and drinking including candy, candied citron, boxes of sweets, coriander, anise water, preserves, pine nut paste, honey water, and sugar cookies.[101] As in *Libro de buen amor*, the author concludes the section by making the connection between fine food, drinking, and lechery: "*Por ende conviene después de mucho comer e de mucho bever muchas diversas e preçiosas viandas luxuria cometer*" (Therefore, after consuming a large variety of expensive foods and drinks, it is likely that one will commit lechery).[102] According to Martínez de Toledo, eating fruits and sweets inevitably leads to wretched excess in all forms.

Hernando de Talavera too condemned excess in all things. His opinion of Muslims as sybaritic was only strengthened by their habit of consuming dried fruits. Figs and raisins, according to Remie Constable, were two markers of Muslim cuisine. In her article about Enrique IV, she writes that "the King enjoyed foods such as figs, raisins, butter, milk, and honey," preferring customs of Moors to those of the Christian religion.[103] Eating quantities of dried fruits was seen as gluttonous because of the pleasure that could be had by sweet tastes.[104] Sinful eating led to avarice, pride, and lust according to Talavera.[105]

From Aldonza's list of sweets in *La Lozana Andaluza*, fried dough, nuts, and honey are the main ingredients of the desserts she remembers fondly: "honeyed fritters, cakes filled with almond paste, toasted hemp seeds and sesame seeds, nougats, fried cakes dipped in honey, flaky pastries, twisted croquettes fried in olive oil, porridge made with almond meal and sorghum."[106] The link between Aldonza's sexual prowess (she is a prostitute) and the luxurious aspects of the foods she remembers makes another connection between Muslim food and lasciviousness.[107]

Although many Christian moralists praised the devout Christian who eschewed pleasurable foods, paradoxically, paradise in all three religions is described in terms of sweets and fruits (see figure 4.3). Biblical references to the land of Canaan in Exodus 3:8 and 13:5 refer to it as the land of milk and honey. Remie Constable writes that "one of the images of Islam that most fascinated medieval Christians was the vision of a sensual Muslim paradise characterized by rivers of milk and honey and inhabited by beautiful young women."[108] The postlapsarian Garden of Eden, as described above by Berceo, is filled with fruit trees. The Qur'an has specific descriptions of the Hereafter in which multiple gardens produce "every kind of fruit." The Qur'an specifically mentions dates (palm trees) and pomegranates (Sura 55:68).

The fig features prominently in religious symbolism and has been associated with both moral and immoral properties. Both the Old and New Testaments make multiple references to figs. Some depictions of the Tree of Knowledge are of a fig tree rather than an apple tree. The reference to the fig leaf is one of shame and lust, but like the pomegranate, figs may also signify fertility. In

Figure 4.3 *The Garden of Eden* **(last quarter of the sixteenth century).** *Source*: Metropolitan Museum of Art, gift of Irwin Untermyer, 1964.

the Song of Songs, a multitude of sweets and fruits are likened to love and pleasure: 2:5 reads, "Sustain me with raisins/refresh me with apples, for I am faint with love,"[109] and 5:1, "I have come to my garden, My sister, my bride; I gather my myrrh with my spice, I eat my honeycomb with my honey, I drink my wine with my milk. Eat, friends, drink, and be drunk with love."[110]

Fruits, then, maintain a complex relationship with the Christian moralists of the Middle Ages. Although many fruits were considered paradisiacal, others were thought to be ruinous to one's moral health. On the other hand, Muslims and Jews gloried in the delight of fruits, nuts, and sweets. Their consumption was not tainted with the condemnation of physical pleasures. Van Gelder writes that Islamic morality tales recommending moderation and condemning overeating were more common than total abstinence or starvation.[111] The concept of eschewing all pleasurable foods, however, was a Christian attitude that became more fraught with anxiety as the need to separate oneself religiously as well as culturally from the Jews and Muslims became a life-or-death decision in the fifteenth century.

Among the wealthy, fruits and sweets were part of their daily consumption of foods. Looking back at the household of Marie d'Anjou, we see that of the 243 pounds spent on foodstuffs, 9 pounds were spent on spices (including cinnamon and cloves) and 4 pounds were spent on fresh and dried fruits.[112] Fresh fruit, made into jams and syrups, was more common among lower classes than sugary sweets. But sweets made with fried dough and honey, as we saw in many of the cooking manuals of the time, were quite common, especially during holidays.

Medieval Christian moralists may have been correct in their assertions that the consumption of sugar would lead to sin, but perhaps not in the ways that they imagined. The production of sugar became one of the most immoral businesses in the history of globalized commerce. The first cane grown in the Mediterranean basin was produced across North Africa and on a number of Mediterranean Islands including Sicily. However, production in the Mediterranean gave way to growth in the Atlantic islands of Spain and Portugal including Madeira, the Canaries, and Sao Tomé.[113]

Christopher Columbus brought sugar cane to the New World on his second voyage, and the rest, as they say, is history. Although early production of sugar cane prospered in the colonies of Spain, ultimately it was France, Britain, and the Netherlands that became the sugar-producing countries.[114] With the demand for sugar increasing throughout the world, the labor involved in sugar production created an ever-increasing demand for enslaved Africans.

The production of sugar in the Mediterranean became more common in the fifteenth century, yet most people did not have access to this sweetener. Sugar was, in the Middle Ages, mainly for the classes who could afford small luxuries. The demand for sugar did not grow until the sixteenth century when the industrialization of sugar production became the norm.

By the sixteenth century, "the medical uses of sugar had become widely established in Europe."[115] There were, however, many physicians who maintained a healthy suspicion toward the miraculous powers of sugar. These physicians commented on the tie between consumption of sugar and rotting teeth and the connection between blood diseases and sugar.[116]

The consumption of sugar grew as importation became easier throughout the Western world. The association with the consumption of sugar and its use in a variety of drinks, including tea, coffee, and chocolate, along with the production of rum, made sugar an indispensable commodity across the trading empires of Spain, England, France, The Netherlands, and other competing countries.[117] The trade of enslaved peoples grew exponentially throughout the West Indies in order to satisfy the sweet tooth of the European market.[118]

In the Middle Ages, fruits and sweets constituted part of the simple pleasures of life. For the poorer classes, sugar was unattainable, but honey provided a satisfying sweetener, and the cookbooks of the time demonstrate the ubiquity of honey in both sweet and savory dishes. Dried fruits were a luxury and rarely seen in poorer households. Pastries and sweets made of fried dough and covered with honey were the most common treats among the lower classes. Muslims became famous in the Middle Ages for their buñuelos, or fried doughnuts. So much so, that to be a *buñolero* in the fifteenth century was to be identified as a Muslim or a *morisco*.

One of the reasons that Pedro Aznar Cardona used to explain his justification of the expulsion of the *moriscos* in the early seventeenth century was their continued affinity toward fruits and sweets. He writes: "*Con este pan, los que podían, juntaban, pasas, higos, miel, arrope, leche, y frutas a su tiempo como melones, aunque fuesen verdes o no mayores que un puño, pepinos, duraznos, y otras cualesquiera"* (With this bread, those who were able, combined raisins, figs, honey, syrup, milk and ripe fruits like melons, even those that were green or not completely ripe, cucumbers, peaches, and whatever else).[119]

Although the consumption of sweets and fruit was not considered sinful among Jews or Muslims, Christians condemned the overconsumption of these pleasurable items as both immoral and non-Christian.

NOTES

1. Thomas Glick, *Islamic and Christian Spain in the Early Middle Ages* (Leiden: Brill, 2005), 79.

2. James Anderson, *Daily Life during the Spanish Inquisition* (Westport, CT: Greenwood Press, 2002), 190.

3. Tomás Puñal Fernández, *El mercado en Madrid en la Baja Edad Media* (Madrid: Caja de Madrid, 1992), 240.

4. R. Dozy, ed., *Le Calendrier de Cordoue*, trans. Charles Pellat (Leiden: E.J. Brill, 1961), 36.

5. Dozy, *Le Calendrier*, 48.

6. Dozy, *Le Calendrier*, 60.

7. Dozy, *Le Calendrier*, 76.

8. The growing of grapes and the consumption of wine will be discussed at length in chapter 5.

9. Dozy, *Le Calendrier*, 88.

10. Dozy, *Le Calendrier*, 102–3.

11. Dozy, *Le Calendrier*, 117–18.

12. Dozy, *Le Calendrier*, 130–31.

13. Dozy, *Le Calendrier*, 144.

14. Dozy, *Le Calendrier*, 158.

15. Dozy, *Le Calendrier*, 172.

16. Juan de Aviñon, *Sevillana Medicina* (Sevilla: Enrique Rasco, 1885), 74.

17. Aviñon, *Sevillana Medicina*, 76.

18. Aviñon, *Sevillana Medicina*, 79.

19. Aviñon, *Sevillana Medicina*, 79.

20. Aviñon, *Sevillana Medicina*, 80–81.

21. Expiración García Sánchez, "La alimentación popular urbana en al-Andalus," *Arqueología medieval* 4 (1996): 230.

22. Aviñon, *Sevillana Medicina*, 76–77.

23. Moses Maimonides, *Medical Aphorisms Treatises 1–5*, trans. Gerrit Bos (Salt Lake City: Brigham Young University Press, 2004), 89.

24. Aviñon, *Sevillana Medicina*, 84–86.

25. Maimonides, *Medical Aphorisms*, 89.

26. Arnaldo de Vilanova, *Régimen de Salud*, ed. Juan Cruz Cruz (Huesca, Spain: La Val de Onsera, 1997), 122.

27. Vilanova, *Régimen de Salud*, 123.

28. García Sánchez, *La alimentación popular*, 230.

29. 'Abd al-Rahmān ibn Muhammad ibn Wāfid, *Tratado de agricultura*, trans. Cipriano Cuadrado Romero (Málaga: Analecta Malacitana, 1997), 55.

30. José Pérez Vidal, *Medicina y dulcería en el Libro de buen amor* (Madrid: Cupsa Editorial, 1981), 23.

31. Expiración García Sánchez, "El sabor de lo dulce en la gastronomía andalusí," *La herencia árabe en la agricultura y el bienestar de Occidente*, ed. Fernando Nuez Viñals (Valeñcia: Universidad Politécnica de Valencia, 2002), 176.

32. García Sánchez, "El sabor de lo dulce," 179.

33. Adela Fábregas García, "El azúcar de caña en el mundo mediterráneo medieval," *Andalucía en la historia*, no. 45 (2014): 46.

34. García Sánchez, "El sabor de lo dulce," 196.

35. García Sánchez, "El sabor de lo dulce," 179.

36. Tsugitaka Sato, *Sugar in the Social Life of Medieval Islam* (Leiden: Brill, 2015), 92.

37. Sato, *Sugar in the Social Life of Medieval Islam*, 92–103 passim.

38. Pérez Vidal, *Medicina y dulcería*, 36.

39. Juan Ruiz, *The Book of Good Love*, trans. Elizabeth Drayson MacDonald, ed. Melveena McKendrick (London: Everyman, 1999), 330, st. 1337.

40. Ruiz, *The Book of Good Love*, 331, st. 1337.

41. Carles Vela, "Defining 'Apothecary' in the Medieval Crown of Aragon," in *Medieval Urban Identity: Health, Economy and Regulation*, ed. Flocel Sabaté (Newcastle upon Tyne: Cambridge Scholars, 2015), 137.

42. Alicia Martínez Crespo, ed., *Manual de mugeres en el qual se contienen muchas y diversas reçeutas muy buenas* (Salamanca: Universidad de Salamanca, 1995), 71.

43. Martínez Crespo, *Manual de mugeres*, 51.

44. Joan Santanach, ed., *The Book of Sent Soví: Medieval Recipes from Catalonia*, trans. Robin Vogelzang (Barcelona: Barcino-Tamesis, 2014), 135.

45. Santanach, *The Book of Sent Soví*, 137.

46. David M. Gitlitz and Linda Kay Davidson, *A Drizzle of Honey: The Lives and Recipes of Spain's Secret Jews* (New York: St. Martin's Press, 1999), 135–39.

47. Ibn Razīn al-Tugībī, *Relieves de las mesas, acerca de las delicias de la comida y los diferentes platos*, ed. and trans. Manuela Marín (Gijón, Spain: Ediciones Trea, 2007), 143–45.

48. Al-Tugībī, *Relieves de las mesas*, 162–63.

49. Al-Tugībī, *Relieves de las mesas*, 221–25.

50. Carolyn A. Nadeau, *Food Matters: Alonso Quijano's Diet and the Discourse of Early Modern Spain* (Toronto: University of Toronto Press, 2016), 130.

51. Santanach, *The Book of Sent Soví*, 129.

52. Ruberto de Nola, *Libro de cozina* (Barcelona: Paneuropea de Ediciones y Publicaciones, 1972), 95.

53. Martínez Crespo, *Manual de mugeres*, 57.

54. Martínez Crespo, *Manual de mugeres*, 59.

55. García Sánchez, "El sabor de lo dulce," 186.

56. Gitlitz and Davidson, *A Drizzle of Honey*, 264.

57. García Sánchez, "El sabor de lo dulce," 193.

58. Al-Tugībī, *Relieves de las mesas*, 45.

59. Gitlitz and Davidson, *A Drizzle of Honey*, 252.

60. Gitlitz and Davidson, *A Drizzle of Honey*, 252.

61. Stephen Nichols, "Seeing Food: An Anthropology of Ekphrasis, and Still Life in Classical and Medieval Examples," *MLN* 106 (1991): 849.

62. Gonzalo de Berceo, *Milagros de Nuestra Señora*, ed. Michael Gerli (Madrid: Cátedra, 1988), 70, st. 4.

63. Gonzalo de Berceo, "The Miracles of Our Lady," *The Collected Works of Gonzalo de Berceo*, trans. Jeannie K. Bartha, Annette Grant Cash, and Richard Terry Mount (Tempe: Arizona Center for Medieval and Renaissance Studies, 2008), 13, st. 4.

64. Berceo, *Milagros*, 72, st. 15.

65. Berceo, "The Miracles," 14–15, st. 15.

66. Berceo, *Milagros*, 76, st. 39.

67. Berceo, "The Miracles," 18, st. 39.

68. www.myjewishlearning.com/article/9-jewish-things-about-pomegranates.

69. Patricia Langley, "Why a Pomegranate?" *BMJ: British Medical Journal* 321, no. 7269 (November 4, 2000): 1154.

70. http://umich.edu/~umfandsf/symbolismproject/symbolism.html/index.html.

71. Berceo, *Milagros*, 100, st. 162.

72. Berceo, "The Miracles," 37, st. 162.

73. Berceo, "The Miracles," 37n3.

74. Berceo, *Milagros*, 123, st. 298.

75. Berceo, "The Miracles," 59, st. 298.

76. Berceo, "The Miracles," 59n10.

77. Ruiz, *The Book of Good Love*, 212, st. 862.

78. Ruiz, *The Book of Good Love*, 213, st. 862.

79. Ruiz, *The Book of Good Love*, 212, l. 867b.

80. Ruiz, *The Book of Good Love*, 213, l. 867b.

81. Ruiz, *The Book of Good Love*, 319–21, st. 1288–90.

82. Ruiz, *The Book of Good Love*, 320, st. 1291.

83. Ruiz, *The Book of Good Love*, 321, st. 1291.

84. María Jesús Rubiera Mata, "La dieta de Ibn Quzmān: Notas sobre la alimentación andalusí a través de su literatura," in *La alimentación en las culturas islámicas,* ed. Manuela Marín and David Waines (Madrid: Agencia Española de Cooperación Internacional, 1994), 132.

85. Ibn Quzmān, *Cancionero andalusí*, ed. Federico Corriente (Madrid: Ediciones Hiperión, 1996), 77, st. 6.

86. Ibn Quzmān, *Cancionero andalusí*, 270.

87. Ibn Quzmān, *Cancionero andalusí*, 91, ll. 5cd.

88. Ibn Quzmān, *Cancionero andalusí*, 53–54.

89. Peter Cole, ed. and trans., *The Dream of the Poem: Hebrew Poetry from Muslim and Christian Spain 950–1492* (Princeton: Princeton University Press, 2007), 122.

90. Cole, *The Dream of the Poem*, 133.

91. *Sefaria: A Living Library of Jewish Texts*, accessed November 9, 2020, www.sefaria.org/texts, Song of Songs 2:3.

92. Cole, *The Dream of the Poem*, 143.

93. Cole, *The Dream of the Poem*, 146–47.

94. Raymond P. Scheindlin, *Wine, Women and Death: Medieval Hebrew Poems on the Good Life* (Oxford: Oxford University Press, 1986), 103.

95. Nichols, "Seeing Food," 849.

96. Ruiz, *The Book of Good Love*, 80, st. 294.

97. Ruiz, *The Book of Good Love*, 81, st. 294.

98. Ruiz, *The Book of Good Love*, 80, st. 296.

99. Ruiz, *The Book of Good Love*, 81, st. 296.

100. Alfonso Mártinez de Toledo, *Arcipreste de Talavera o Corbacho,* ed. Michael Gerli (Madrid: Cátedra, 1998), 130–31.

101. Mártinez de Toledo, *Arcipreste de Talavera o Corbacho*, 131.

102. Mártinez de Toledo, *Arcipreste de Talavera o Corbacho*, 131.

103. Olivia Remie Constable, "Food and Meaning: Christian Understandings of Muslim Food and Food Ways in Spain, 1250–1550," *Viator* 44, no. 3, (2013): 200.

104. Remie Constable, "Food and Meaning," 212.

105. Teresa de Castro Martínez, "El gusto en la doctrina moral de la Iglesia en la Baja Edad Media," *Micrologus: Natura, Scienze e Società Medievali* (2002): 390.

106. Quoted in Remie Constable, "Food and Meaning," 218.

107. Remie Constable, "Food and Meaning," 218–19.

108. Remie Constable, "Food and Meaning," 212.

109. http://classic.net.bible.org/verse.php?book=Sos&chapter=2&verse=5.

110. http://classic.net.bible.org/verse.php?book=Sos&chapter=5&verse=1.

111. Geert Jan Van Gelder, *God's Banquet: Food in Classical Arabic Literature* (New York: Columbia University Press, 2000), 34.

112. C. M. Woolgar, "Food and Taste in Europe in the Middle Ages," in *Food: The History of Taste,* ed. Paul Freedman (London: Thames & Hudson, 2007), 181.

113. Sidney Mintz, *Sweetness and Power* (New York: Viking Penguin, 1985), 24.

114. Mintz, *Sweetness and Power*, 35.

115. Mintz, *Sweetness and Power*, 103.

116. Mintz, *Sweetness and Power*, 105.

117. Mintz, *Sweetness and Power*, 108.

118. Mintz, *Sweetness and Power*, 53.

119. Quoted in Remie Constable, "Food and Meaning," 228n146.

Chapter 5

Wine

Wine was as integral to the daily diet of the Middle Ages as bread. Consumed by everyone, including children (well-watered, of course), wine was the most common drink in medieval Iberia. Wine fueled much of the social life in the Middle Ages, both in private residences and in taverns. In the cities, taverns thrived as loci of social interaction mainly for men. Wine drinking parties were common among Muslims and Jews, with reams of poetry written about the joys and sorrows of drinking. Drunkenness, in general, was frowned upon by the tenets of all three religions, although Christians tended toward a more moralistic view of drinking, citing Noah as a prime example of the woes of immoderation.[1]

Wine was an integral part of medical interventions, although as Rose points out, it may have been difficult to distinguish between dietary and medical advice.[2] Medical professionals from all three religions recommended wine as an important element of a healthy diet. Medical treatises recommended wine for a variety of illnesses and humoral imbalances, and medicinal concoctions often called for wine mixed with herbs and spices to cure a variety of ailments. Wine was especially helpful for people suffering from stomach ailments (since the cleanliness of water was not always reliable).[3] Wine was also used as a disinfectant for war wounds.[4]

A family who owned even a small parcel of land would plant their own grapevines. Rose writes that Jews planted vines wherever they lived. Their consumption ranged from 1.5 to 3 liters per day.[5] There are a number of references to personal vineyards, presses, and wine cellars in private documents of the eleventh and twelfth centuries, before regulation of the wine trade became an economic expedient. Rose writes that exportation of wine from the Iberian Peninsula to England, France, and Flanders dates at least from the thirteenth century.[6]

There were a number of ways one could acquire wine. The majority of wine was sold in a centralized market space or the main plaza. Other venues included stores, vintners' houses, and taverns.[7] Taverns and hostels were common in most medium-sized towns.[8] However, the popularity of taverns with those less than desirable members of society made their existence problematic throughout medieval Iberia. Laws were created to ensure that taverns could coexist with their neighbors. Some of these laws required that all unseemly activities stay within the walls of the tavern. Fines would be charged for any activities spilling out into the streets.[9] Laws were also created to ensure that members of the drinking public were not defrauded by tavern owners looking to increase their revenues.[10] Women did not drink in public unless they were of low moral character.[11] In general, taverns were not looked upon favorably as they were centers of bad behavior. That aside, taverns were, as one could imagine, popular places to imbibe with friends (see figure 5.1).

The vineyards that had been established by the Romans continued to flourish in the Middle Ages. Although the assumption was that most wine was consumed by Jews and Christians, Glick writes that there was a "tremendous market for grapes, raisins and wine among Muslims as well" due to Iraqi influence during the reign of Abd al-Rahman II.[12] It was during his reign (CE 822–852) that the cultural environment of Córdoba grew to splendid heights. Wine drinking was just one aspect of this "emerging elite culture of al-Andalus."[13] Drinking would become much more problematic during the rule of the Almoravids

Figure 5.1.   A tavern scene by the Flemish baroque artist Adriaen Brouwer, c. 1635.

starting in the eleventh century. Amira Bennison writes that the "Almoravids were invited into al-Andalus by a population, sick of their wine-swilling and ineffectual Ta'ifa rulers."[14] Irreligious habits like wine drinking were seriously discouraged. However, if we take Ibn Quzmān and other Arab poets at their word, the habit did not disappear even under the most disapproving of leaders.

The consumption of wine was often fraught with religious anxiety. Medieval Rabbis maintained strict restrictions against wine that was not produced by Jews. Although most wine produced by Christians was for general consumption, strict adherents of Judaism considered all wine produced by gentiles as an "idolatrous libation."[15] Christians were allowed to drink wine produced by Jews or Muslims, and Muslims, who were ostensibly prohibited from drinking, demonstrated their avid interest in wine in poetry and health manuals.

Monasteries kept their own vineyards in order to supply both liturgical and dietary needs of their inhabitants.[16] Tending vineyards was a time-consuming and labor-intensive process. By the thirteenth century, monasteries and lay lords in the north had to begin paying their laborers because it was difficult to find enough peasants to tend the vineyards.[17]

Ruiz outlines the four major labors of the vineyard: *excavar*, to loosen a weed growth; *podar*, to trim vines; *cavar*, to dig; and *vendimiar*, to gather grapes.[18] Ibn Wāfid details the exact methodology behind growing the best grapes in his *Tratado de Agricultura*. His instructions range from the kinds of soil into which each varietal of grape should be planted, to the depth of the hole for each vine shoot. In chapter 15, titled "*Cómo saben escoger los lugares para poner las viñas*" ("How to Know Where to Put the Vines"), Ibn Wāfid writes that green or white grapes should be planted in humid land near spring water, whereas dry, sandy soil is best for red or purple grapes.[19] In chapter 17, "*Cómo se ponen las viñas*" ("How to Plant the Vines"), he tells us that vines should be planted in holes of "six palms" if the vines are on hilly lands, and in holes of "three to four palms" on flatlands.[20]

In the *Calendario de Córdoba*, pruning the vines, the ripening process, pressing and picking the grapes are all activities that are mentioned throughout the year. In January, vines should be ready for pruning and grafting.[21] In April and May, the grapes ripen.[22] June sees the preparation of verjuice, a juice made from pressing unripe grapes, which was used like vinegar (see figure 5.2).[23] In July, grapes have ripened and are ready to be picked (see figure 5.3).[24]

Wine was considered an indispensable element of the daily diet and an important ingredient in pharmaceuticals. Aviñon writes, "*El vino es vianda y es melezina y esfuerça las virtudes todas súbitamente y penetra luego el coraçon y es caliente y es fria, y deseca y da humidad*" (Wine is both food and medicine, it strengthens virtues and penetrates the heart, it is warm and

Figure 5.2 Picking green grapes to make verjuice. *Source*: From the *Tacuinum sanitatis*, MS Paris 9333 (BNF, Paris) 1445–1451.

cool, dry, and wet).[25] Much of the medicinal mixtures of the Middle Ages contained some form of wine. Through Juan de Aviñon's discussion of the health risks and benefits of the different varietals of wine available in the fourteenth century, we know the kinds of wines that were easily accessible: red and white, sweet, and dry, aged and new. Rose also mentions Madeira, spiced wine, and wine made from raisins.[26]

Aviñon lays out the requirements for the most complete daily diet, which includes "quatro libras de vianda" (four pounds of food):

> *Pongo una libra de pan y dos de carne, ques una libra carnicera, y una de vino, que es medio acçumbre, medio a la mañana y medio a la noche; . . . y como quier que en el vino se eche agua non es de contar, porque el agua non da nudrimento, según dicho de los doctores.*[27]
>
> ----
>
> One should eat one pound of bread, two pounds of meat, and one of wine (half in the morning and half in the evening); . . . one may water the wine, but this does not count since, according to medical men, water does not have any nutritional value.

Figure 5.3   Picking grapes to make wine. *Source*: From the abridged Latinized MS Rome 4182 housed in the Biblioteca Casanatense in Rome, 1390–1400 (Cat. MS 4182).

Aviñon describes a number of factors that should be considered when drinking wine for one's health including the color of the grape (white, red, purple), the age of the wine, the sweetness or dryness of the wine, and recipes for medicinal concoctions. When considering the kinds and amounts of wine, the humoral nature of the imbiber is also vitally important.[28]

The manual is exhaustive in its detailing of the qualities of wine and its varietals. Young wine, for example, must be made from the green grape. Its color, aroma, and taste must be light and pleasing. Young wine is useful for those of both a warm and cool humoral nature: it cools the hot natured and warms the cold natured and also aids in digestion.[29] The manual does warn, however, that wine should not be drunk "*sin razón*" (without reason), because it turns men into beasts.[30] It turns out that red wine is good for cold folks and old folks but bad for those of a fiery temperament. Aviñon cites Ibn Sina on the proportions of water to wine and recommends that most wine be watered to prevent drunkenness.[31]

Aviñon also includes electuaries in the section on wine. These aforementioned medicinal concoctions often had wine as their base ingredient. Recipes could have as many as twenty ingredients and contained very complex instructions. One recipe, for "pepper wine," which, according to the manual, was helpful for those of a phlegmatic temperament and also to take during the winter months, calls for ginger, pepper, galangal, nutmeg, cinnamon, cloves, and plants such as spikenard and sedge. The recipe also calls for a half liter of white wine mixed with honey.[32] Vilanova also discusses wine at length in his treatise. The variations of wine in the *Dietética medieval* include raisin wine as a laxative and also to ease a cough; anise wine for nursing mothers; and fennel wine, which, according to Rose, could have been used "as an abortifacient."[33]

Wine is mentioned in the health manuals of both Muslim and Jewish medical men. Although it was generally understood that Muslims were not allowed to drink intoxicants, David Waines points out that the punishment for drunkenness is not explicitly mentioned in the Qur'an.[34] Muslim medical treatises, like their Christian counterparts, discussed the benefits of alcohol. In his article on the ninth-century Persian physician Abū Bakr al-Rāzī's contemporary Abu Zayd al-Balkhī, Waines cites both clinician's views on the consumption of alcohol. Waines writes that al-Rāzī's chapter declaring the benefits of "intoxicating drinks" has been excised from the most modern edition of his book on dietetics, demonstrating a hardened view of "religious deviance."[35] Al-Rāzī, mentioned earlier in this book, wrote, "Intoxicating drinks warm the body and set about helping digest the food in the stomach, hastening its penetration of the kidney and its digestion there, spreading thence through the veins to the rest of the body."[36] The general word *sharāb* is used throughout the treatise, which means any type of drink. However, Waines points out that in al-Balkhī's treaty, *sharāb* is a "culinary substitute for the life-giving element of water."[37] The Spanish word *jarabe* and the English words "shrub" and "syrup" are derived from this word. These derivatives can be alcoholic or nonalcoholic, which leaves the interpretation of the word *sharāb* unclear. Based on the rest of the medical texts, however, *sharāb* meant some form of wine.

Like the *Sevillana Medicina*, al-Rāzī's treatise explains the use of different varietals of wine based on humoral temperaments. However, al-Rāzī also discusses the consumption of date and raisin wine. For phlegmatics, the best wine is made of honey and raisins, and for moist temperaments, date wine is recommended.[38] Christian manuals ignore the existence of date wine, but for Muslims, date wine became the focus of some religious attention, which is discussed later in the chapter.

Maimonides recommended wine to balance one's temperament and to evacuate bad humors.[39] Thin wine is good for digestion and fortification.[40] Generally, Maimonides warns against water in favor of wine. The situation in which Maimonides found himself, a Jew as physician to the Sultan Saladin, demonstrates the differences in the religious implications of wine in the Middle Ages. When asked to suggest a cure for the Sultan's nephew, who suffered from depression, Maimonides recommended wine and song. In his justification, Maimonides wrote the following:

> Our Master should not criticize his humble servant for having mentioned in this treatise the use of wine and songs, both of which are abhorred by the religion. For this servant did not command acting in this manner; he merely stated that which is dictated by his profession. Indeed, the religious legislators know, as do the physicians, that wine has benefits for man. A physician is bound, inasmuch as he is a physician, to present with a beneficial regimen, whether it is forbidden or permitted; the patient is endowed with the freedom to choose whether to follow or not. If [the physician] fails to mention everything that may be helpful, be it forbidden or permitted, he is guilty of acting dishonestly, for he did not offer trustworthy advice.[41]

The consensus among medical men at the time was that wine was essential for good health. Among women homemakers and healers, wine was also used in a variety of medicinal and hygienic mixtures. One, titled "*remedio para las muelas*" (remedy for molars), calls for white wine mixed with the nut of the cypress tree, dried roses, cherry plums, alum, and honey. Other mixtures calling for white wine were to keep the teeth, hands, and face clean.[42]

In Christian food manuals, wine, and its nonalcoholic cousin verjuice, were used as dressing, sauce, and marinade. In the *Sent Soví*, a recipe for asparagus calls for the vegetable to be fried first and then dressed with a mixture of wine, herbs, and a little sugar.[43] For a roasted chicken, verjuice is added to a mixture of "good spices" to be added to the blended livers as a type of gravy.[44] For "piglet pluck," "strong wine" is recommended for the sauce.[45]

In Nola's *Libro de cozina*, a sweet sauce used for all types of poultry calls for bread, sweet red wine, black grapes, and a large number of raisins. A liver recipe in *A Drizzle of Honey* calls for sherry or other sweet wines. This recipe is based, according to Gitlitz and Davidson, on a recipe found in Nola's manual. "Juana Nuñez's Meat and Eggplant Stew" calls for both red wine and strong vinegar.[46] Many recipes call for the addition of acid as a finishing touch. This acid often came in the form of vinegar or verjuice.

Vinegar is one of the most commonly used condiments in *Relieves de las mesas*.[47] The varieties that Ibn Razīn calls for include *vinagre blanco* and *vinagre dulce* (white or sweet vinegar), but no recipes call for *vinagre de vino* (wine vinegar). Verjuice, lemon juice, lime juice, and other juices made from citrus fruits and herbs are used throughout the manual.[48] Ibn Razīn also devotes an entire chapter to pickled foods, including olives, capers, eggplants, and limes.[49]

WINE IN LITERATURE

In literature, wine and drinking were subject to drunken adulation and moral condemnation. Berceo and Juan Ruiz, like the Christian moralists of the time, believed that overconsumption of wine led to gluttony and lust, although the tone in *Libro de buen amor* is more jocular. The Hebrew and Arabic literary traditions of wine poetry, however, celebrate wine: how it looks, how it smells, how it tastes, and how it feels when one has drunk sufficiently. Even though Muslims were prohibited from drinking, the quantity of wine poetry produced in the Middle Ages demonstrates the differences between religious law and daily practice.

In texts with a more religious purpose, wine often represented the blood of Christ—an integral part of Christian mass and communion service. The concept of transubstantiation, although one that was part of Christian religious ritual well before the Fourth Lateran Council's formal definition in 1215, is an essential part of the literature of Berceo. In the *Milagros*, as discussed in the chapter on bread, Christ's body is often referred to with grain and bread metaphors. Not surprisingly, however, Berceo refers to wine only as a drink that should be avoided. In the more liturgical *Sacrificio de la misa*, Berceo speaks to his audience about bread and wine as body and blood. Kevin Poole writes that Berceo's emphasis on the transformation of bread and wine in *Sacrificio de la misa* demonstrates a personal devotion to the concept of transubstantiation that precedes any statement made by Pope Innocent during the Lateran Council declaring the "Real Presence" of Christ in the communion ritual.[50]

The Virgin Mary is associated with grapes (and other fruits) throughout the *Milagros*. In the description of the postlapsarian Eden that serves as an introduction to the collection of tales, Berceo gives the reader a number of names for Mary, including "Vine" and "Grape": *"Es dicha vid, es uva."*[51] Mary is also called a "grapevine" that grows on the arbor (Christ): *"asentó buena vinna cerca de buen parral."*[52] Traditionally, Christ is the Vine, yet Berceo associates Mary with both fruit and vine in this section; an association that indicates that she is both the progenitor of the grape (Christ) and fruit of God's garden.

Berceo condemns drunkenness as a pathway to Hell in miracle XX, titled "El monje embriagado" (The Inebriated Monk). In this tale, the monk has spent much of his evening drinking:

Entró enna bodega   un día por ventura,
bebió mucho del vino,   esto fo sin mesura,
embebdóse el locco,   issió de su cordura,
yogó hasta las viésperas   sobre la tierra dura.[53]

He entered the wine cellar by chance one day;
he drank a great deal of wine: this was without moderation.
The crazy man got drunk: he took leave of his senses;
until vespers he lay on the hard ground.[54]

Berceo equates drinking with losing one's senses. As the medical men of
Berceo's time warn against drinking "*sin razón*" (without reason), so too does
Berceo warn against drinking as dangerous for one's soul. When the monk
awakens, he is, if not still inebriated, then terribly hungover. Pedro Pinero
Ramírez writes that this tale describes the first *delirium tremens* in Spanish
literature.[55] The Devil sees his opportunity to "trip up" the monk by throwing
a number of obstacles at him on his way to church. He first appears to the
monk in the form of a bull:

En figura de toro   que es escalentado,
cavando con los piedes,   el cejo demudado,
con fiera conadura,   sannoso e irado,
paróseli delante   el traïdor provado.[56]

In the form of a bull that is raging,
pawing the ground with his hooves, with changed countenance,
with fierce horns, angry and irate,
    the proven traitor stopped before him.[57]

The Virgin Mary protects the monk from being gored by the bull. The
Devil (the "proven traitor") tries twice more to prevent the monk from enter-
ing into the church—once as a rabid dog and again as a fierce lion. The Virgin
Mary manages to clear the poor monk's path so that he may enter the church.
She also helps him home to sleep off the effects and encourages him to con-
fess, which he most assuredly does.

There are multiple sections of *Libro de buen amor* in which wine plays a
prominent role. Given much of the text's ribald nature, the reader might expect
some positive depictions of wine. However, wine tends to be portrayed in the
text in a relatively negative light. In one section of the text titled, "*De commo
el Amor castiga al Arçipreste que aya en sy buenas constunbres, e ssobr todo
que se guarde de beuer mucho vino blanco e tynto*" ("How Love Advises the
Archpriest to Behave Respectably and Above All Not to Drink Too Much Red
and White Wine"), Lord Love warns the archpriest that overindulgence of wine
will lead to covetousness, lust, and pride. The first stanza in this section reads:

Buenas costunbres deues en ty syenpre aver,
guardate sobre todo mucho vino beuer,
que el vino fizo a loc con sus fijas boluer,

en verguença del mundo, en saña de dios caer.[58]

You must always behave properly,
and above all avoid drinking too much wine,
Wine drove Lot to lie with his daughters, and brought
the shame of the world and the anger of God upon him.[59]

Other stanzas warn that drinking to excess leads to a shortened life, foul breath, and loss of common sense. At the end of the section Lord Love declares:

Es el vino muy bueno en su mesma natura,
muchas bondades tiene sy se toma con mesura,
Al que demas lo veue sacalo de cordura,
toda maldat del mundo fase e toda locura.[60]

In itself wine is a good thing,
bringing many blessings if drunk in moderation,
but a man who drinks too much loses his good sense,
and brings about all the evil and madness in the world.[61]

Other sections in which wine plays a role include scenes of feasting, gluttony, and sexual encounters. Prior to the battle of Lent and Carnal, Lord Carnal throws a large banquet for all of his troops. During this feast, wine flows freely, allowing the troops to forget what lies before them: "*Tañia amenudo con el el añafyl;/parlaua mucho el vino, de todos alguaçil*"[62] ("The goblet sounded often on the wood of the barrel,/the wine spoke at length, as it was everyone's beadle"[63]). When Lady Lent attacks Lord Carnal's troops, they are ill-prepared and hungover. Their inevitable defeat leads to forty days of Lent and Lord Carnal's penitential diet. Although wine was not forbidden during Lent, Lord Carnal's diet was prescribed with his particular sins in mind, therefore he was allowed only water (see figure 5.4).

The association of wine and lust led to Christian condemnation of drunkenness. Muslim and Hebrew wine poetry centered on the notion of wine as one of life's pleasures but did so in a less judgmental way. Wine drinking parties in Muslim Iberia have been well chronicled. These parties were made up of courtiers and other members of the aristocracy. Along with wine, revelers were entertained by music, dancing, and the participation of the wine drinkers themselves in composing spontaneous verse, often entering into competitions for the wittiest verse. These wine parties often took place out of doors, under the night sky. Wine pourers, known as *sakis*, were usually prepubescent boys or young girls, dressed as boys. The *saki* was often the subject of erotic verse composed during these parties.

Figure 5.4 Miniature of a scene in a tavern illustrating gluttony with men drinking, and below a cellarer passing up a drink. *Source*: Image taken from *Treatise on the Vices* (late fourteenth century). British Library.

Raymond Scheindlin writes that much of the poetry was political and satirical in nature. However, light verse was composed among the courtier class for simple amusement.[64] Scheindlin focuses on the Hebrew poets of Andalucía who stand out as masters of the rhetorical and rhythmical standards of the "Golden Age" of Hebrew poetry (between the eleventh and twelfth centuries). Scheindlin tells us that Jews held wine drinking parties and even mixed with Muslims in their parties. According to Scheindlin, two categories of writing appear in wine poems: descriptive and meditative. Descriptive focuses on the wine's appearance, aroma, the cup, the texture, and even the *saki* who serves the wine. The meditative poems focus on the poet's inner world, evoking joy, sorrow, sensuality, and opulence.[65]

The conflict between the temporal and spiritual worlds appears in much of the Hebrew wine poetry. Although the conflict is even greater in the Arabic poetry because of the prohibition of wine by religious law, the concept of "participating in the pleasures of the dominant culture" tinges the Hebrew wine poetry with sadness.[66] Both Hebrew and Arabic wine poetry of medieval

Iberia demonstrate, on one hand, disloyalty to one's religion through imbibing forbidden food and drink, participating in illicit sexual acts, and generally enjoying oneself among the enemy and, on the other, the inevitable chasm between religious and social rules and daily practices.

Al-Harizi's gate 27, "Of the Cup's Joys and Other Alloys," demonstrates the dilemma that exists among those who consider wine drinking pleasurable yet morally problematic. Hever the Kenite displays such rhetorical prowess in his poetic call for abstention that the listeners (in the tavern) throw down their wine and swear off drinking "in perpetuity."[67] He sings:

The knowing eye sees through the veil,
straight to the face of the vine's foul daughter.
Ambrosial her liquors to sotted tongues
but spurned by the wise as muddied water.[68]

Hever claims that wine is the seed of all evil, the "brew of the devil" that drives the sane man insane, ruining his reputation and his health.[69] David Simha Segal writes that despite Hever's rhetorical success against tippling, the reader is left "with unresolved tensions between preachment and the celebration of worldly joys."[70] This mixed message is common throughout the tradition of Hebrew wine poetry.

The themes of Hebrew wine poetry range from physical descriptions of the wine itself, to the melancholic nature of the wine drinker. The juxtaposition of pleasure (wine, beauty, nature) and pain, both physical and metaphysical, is common. Samuel the Nagid (d. 1055 or 1056), the vizier of the ruler of Granada and, according to Scheindlin, "the most powerful Jew in the Middle Ages,"[71] praises the essentials of a good life in the following poem:

If you're like me, and want to pour the wine of joy,
    Hear what I have to say.
I'll teach you pleasure's way, though you don't want to hear,
    You friend of sighs and pain.
Five things there are that fill the hearts of men with joy,
    And put my grief to flight:
A pretty girl, a garden, wine, the water's rush
    In a canal, and song.[72]

In another poem he juxtaposes the beauty of a woman and warmth with iciness and violence:

Take from a fawn the crystal filled with blood
    Of grapes, as bright as hailstones filled with fire.
Her lips are a scarlet thread; her kisses, wine;

Her mouth and body wear the same perfume.
Her hands are crystal wands with ruby tips –
She tints her fingers with her victim's blood.[73]

Many poets expressed the "national dilemma" that was enjoying pleasure in the face of the pain that the Jewish community faced daily.[74] In Dunash ben Labrat's poem on the pleasures of life, the last stanza reads: How can we be carefree/Or raise our cups in glee,/When by all men are we/Rejected and despised?[75] Moses (Moshe) ibn Ezra looks to wine for the blessed forgetfulness from the pain of life:

Drink up, my friend, and pour for me, that I
May to the cup surrender all my pain.
And if you see me dying, tell the boy,
"Revive him! Quick! Take up your lute again."[76]

Focusing on sensuality and pleasure, Samuel the Nagid writes:

How exquisite that fawn who woke at night
    To the sound of viol's thrum and tabor's clink,
Who saw the goblet in my hand and said,
    "The grape's blood flows for you between my lips.
            Come, drink."
Behind him stood the moon, a letter C,
    Inscribed on morning's veil in golden ink.[77]

The similarities between Hebrew and Arabic wine poetry are striking. The poetry of Ibn Quzmān illustrates how wine acts as a social lubricator, as a way to forget the ills of society, and to help heal a broken heart. The prohibition against imbibing alcoholic beverages would appear to be less widespread in al-Andalus, at least among the intellectual elite. Although he lived during the reign of the Almoravids in Córdoba, their famed strictness did not seem to affect his love of wine. His poetry demonstrates the failure of the social controls the Almoravids intended during the twelfth century in al-Andalus.[78]

The poet juxtaposes the pleasures of wine with the pain of its absence in the beginning of *zéjel* 5:

El vino me es grato de gustar
y el amante me agrada abrazar.

Este añejo consuela mis penas;
en la ebriedad yo nombro y destituyo,
y cuando me dicen que es ya generoso

me entristece dejarlo, cuando falta.[79]

The taste of wine pleases me
as a lover I enjoy its embrace.

This aged wine allows me to forget my woes.
In drunkenness, I name them and dismiss them
And when I'm told that I have had enough
it saddens me to leave it, and when I have no more.

The physicality of the wine itself is pleasurable, like a lover. The wine helps him to forget the ills of society. The poet understands that drinking does not solve his problems, yet he cannot help but wish for more once the effects of the wine have passed.

In *zéjel* 11, the poet prefers death to a life without wine:

El quedarme sin vinillo es lo que más aborrezco:
es la pero maldición que cumpla en mí Dios, ¡por Mahoma! . . .

Rato sin beber no tengo por hermoso ni gracioso:
¿qué es un día sin desvergüenza, qué es un día sin descaro?
No hay placer que me parezca, ni tranquilidad tampoco
sin que entre mis labios entre con vino borde de vaso.[80]

To be left without wine is what I abhor the most:
it is the worst curse that God can hand out, by the Prophet!

Without drinking, life has no beauty or wit:
What is a day without shamelessness, what is a day without debauchery?
Neither pleasure nor happiness can exist
until a full glass of wine has entered my lips.

Monroe writes that Ibn Quzmān deliberately held up a mirror to society, using shock tactics to unmask corruption.[81] In one poem, the poet describes a tavern scene in which debauchery is celebrated:

My life is spent in dissipation and wantonness!
O joy, I have begun to be a real profligate!
Indeed, it is absurd for me to repent
When my survival without a wee drink would be certain death.
Vino, vino! And spare me what is said;
Verily, I go mad when I lose my restraint!
My slave will be freed, my money irretrievably lost
On the day I am deprived of the cup.
Should I be poured a double measure or a fivefold one,

I would most certainly empty it; if not, fill then the *jarrón*!
Ho! Clink the glasses with us!
Drunkenness, drunkenness! What care we for proper conduct?[82]

The use of the Spanish word *vino* is both for comic effect and to further the association between the poet, who is a sophisticated intellectual, and his rather unsavory companions in the tavern.[83] Wine is both the bringer of great joy but also the bearer of bad tidings. One thirteenth-century poet from Alicante remarked, "In how many taverns have I woken up as dawn was breaking and the dew falling."[84] The conflict that we see in attitudes toward drinking is reflected in a number of religious texts of the Middle Ages.

RELIGIOUS IMPLICATIONS

Inebriation is condemned by all three religions. In Christian doctrine, the consumption of wine is the focus of much discussion. The link to Christ and communion makes wine a sacred drink. But drinking wine in excess leads to lust and indecorous behavior, which is most solemnly condemned by Christian doctrine. The focus of the opprobrium in Christian texts is the concept of gluttonous pleasure as the root of evil.

Christian moralists condemned overindulgence of all things pleasurable. The Catalán monk Francesc Eiximenis wrote an entire treatise on the subject of overindulgence and gluttony. Eiximenis praised fasting as "the mother of intelligence, wisdom, and knowledge."[85] Avoiding the sin of gluttony allowed man to keep sharp witted. Worse, though, than overindulgence of food, is excessive drinking. In the third volume of his text *Lo Crestià* (*The Christian*), Eiximenis writes:

> Spiritually, it destroys in him any common sense and virtue, forcing him to err, disturbing his conscience, and making him commit adultery and homicide. Drunkenness, in short, breeds every sin in the human soul.
>
> In the body as well, the disordered use of wine produces a number of distressing results which render the drunkard loathsome to everyone.[86]

The description of these physical consequences by Eiximenis forms a vivid picture of the infernal fate which awaits the sick and wretched man who is on his way to *delirium tremens*.[87]

The consumption of wine was often associated with wretched excess. However, in literature of a more religious nature, wine is associated with Christ and communion. These associations are clearly delineated in Berceo's *Sacrificio de la Misa*. Although transubstantiation was not an official tenet

of Christianity until the sixteenth century, the number of references to wine
as the blood of Christ in Berceo's text demonstrates that the concepts behind
transubstantiation had become fundamental to thirteenth-century Christians
(see figures 5.5 and 5.6). Stanza 65 reads:

Ofrecer pan e vino   en el sancto altar
ofrenda es auténtica,   non podrié mejorar,
quando con sus discípulos   Christo quiso cenar,
con pan e vino sólo   los quiso comulgar.[88]

The offering of bread and wine at the holy altar
is an authentic offering, it could not be better;
when Christ desired to sup with his disciples,
He wished their Communion to be only bread and wine.[89]

And the first two lines of stanza 142: "*El pan torne en carne, en la que El
murió;/el vino torne sanne, la que nos redemió*"[90] ("That the bread may
become the body in which He died,/that the wine may become the blood that
redeemed us"[91]).

Wine and water represent the intermingling of God and humanity in stanza
61:

El vino significa   a Dios nuestro Señor,
la agua significa   al pueblo pecador;
como estas dos cosas   tornan en un sabor,

Figure 5.5   *Christ in the Winepress*, Austria, c. 1490. *Source*: Kuttenberger Kantionale
(ÖNB Mus. Hs. 15501), fol. 86v. Austrian National Library, Vienna.

Figure 5.6 *The Mystic Winepress*, **Provence (France), 1485–1493.** *Source*: *Bible morali-sée de Philippe le Hardi* (MS. Français No. 167). National Library of France, Paris.

assín torna el ome   con Dios en buen amor.[92]

The wine signifies the Lord our God,
the water signifies sinful humanity;
as those two properties are blended together,
likewise humanity blends lovingly with God.[93]

Berceo cites John 19:34 as scriptural evidence that wine and water go together: *"Demás, quando estava en la cruz desbrazado,/sangne ixió e agua del so diestro costado"*[94] ("Besides, when He hung, arms outstretched, on the cross,/from His right side there flowed both blood and water"[95]).

The presence of Christ in the act of Communion (drinking the wine/blood) mitigates the sinfulness of humanity. However, by the thirteenth century, the laity were no longer receiving wine at communion; the wine was for clergy alone. Rodrigo-Estevan writes that wine could be a way to salvation, but overindulgence led to drunkenness and sin.[96] There was also a great fear that the clumsy unlettered would spill the blood of Christ as they reached for the goblet. Even receiving the host, the most sacred ritual of the Christian mass, became a once-a-year phenomenon for most Christians in the Middle Ages.[97] Gray proclaims the situation incredibly ironic: the more sacred the ritual, the less likely the regular parishioners were to be intimately involved.[98] Canon 21 of the Fourth Lateran Council reads:

> All the faithful of both sexes shall after they have reached the age of discretion faithfully confess all their sins at least once a year to their own (parish) priest and perform to the best of their ability the penance imposed, receiving reverently at least at Easter the sacrament of the Eucharist.[99]

Poole claims that Berceo did not agree with this new policy as he truly believed that communion was the food for the soul for every Christian.[100]

Although drinking alcohol was prohibited in Islam, there are clear indications that the use of alcohol was common among Muslims in medieval Iberia. This is not to say, however, that wine drinking was not a controversial subject. There are treatises that argue for the use of alcohol in certain social situations as well as during the cold winter months. However, even the physicians who call for moderate drinking at certain times of the year warn against the excess of drink. Al-Balkhī's general rule states, "In everything of great worth there is great danger."[101] Drunkenness in Islam does not quite carry the same implication of wantonness and lust that it does in Christianity; however, the Qur'an does say that drunkenness should be punished. Al-Balkhī writes that the "state of drunkenness is worse than that of a man spirit-possessed."[102]

There are multiple verses in the Qur'an that associate the drinking of intoxicants with Satan and with games of chance.

> O ye who believe! Strong drink and games of chance and idols and divining arrows are only an infamy of Satan's handiwork. Leave it aside in order that ye may succeed.[103]
>
> Satan seeketh only to cast among you enmity and hatred by means of strong drink and games of chance, and to turn you from remembrance of Allah and from (His) worship. Will ye then have done?[104]

Ibn Rushd (Averroes) wrote extensively on the question of drink. Although there was no consensus among Islamic jurists on drinking, most believed that the prohibition covered the category of "khamr"—drinks derived from the juice of grapes. Siddiqui writes that the Qur'an mentions *"khamr"* five times both in reference to sin and also as a heavenly drink.[105] Rushd believed that all intoxicating drinks were prohibited. But others believed that the intoxication was prohibited, not the drink itself.[106]

The question of drinks made of other fruits, like dates, was problematic. Verse 16.67 from the Qur'an reads: "And of the fruits of the date-palm, and grapes, whence ye derive strong drink and (also) good nourishment. Lo! therein is indeed a portent for people who have sense."[107] However, Rushd quotes two hadiths that claim that "khamr" comes from grapes, dates, honey, raisins, and wheat. In this case, then, all intoxicants are prohibited. And the reason for the prohibition is that "intoxication prevents the remembrance of God."[108]

As in Christianity, there existed a large gap between the letter of religious law and daily practice. To read the poetry written by some of the greatest Arab poets of medieval Iberia, one could imagine that the prohibition of wine was not taken as seriously as the law demanded. The social importance of drinking, especially among the elite, seems to have outweighed religious condemnation.[109]

In his treatise on health, Maimonides declares wine as "*la mejor de las exquisiteces o alimentos.*"[110] However, what is best for one's health is not always what is best for one's soul. Maimonides, as a physician, put the needs of the body first. In Judaism, wine is an essential element in religious ritual and social engagements. Wine and grapes in the Old Testament are much praised. Without wine there is no Sabbath: "No rejoicing before God is possible except with wine" (*Talmud*, Pesahim 109a).[111] Even in Rabbinical literature, wine drinking (in moderation) is generally seen in a positive light. The first lines of Eruvin 65b read: "This teaches that if wine flows in a person's house like water, there is a blessing, but if not, there is no blessing."[112]

Metaphorically, wine represents the essence of goodness, whereas the wicked are compared to vinegar. In Psalm 128:3, both blessed mothers and wives are compared to fruitful vines:

Your wife will be like a fruitful vine
within your house;
your children shall be like olive shoots
around your table.[113]

In Genesis 49:11, Judah demonstrates his prosperity by washing his garments in wine and his clothes in the blood of grapes.[114]

Noah acts as an example against drunkenness, as he does in Christianity. All three religions condemn the loss of self-control. In Judaism, the imagery of Satan watering Noah's vineyard with animal blood demonstrates how bestial a man can become with drink.[115] The Qur'an condemns drink for its ability to allow man to forget God. And in Christianity, excess of drink allows men to lose themselves in lust and gluttony. Although wine was the most essential drink in medieval Iberia, its consumption was fraught with religious anxiety.

Shards of crystal have been found throughout southern Spain in architectural sites. The vessel with which wine was consumed by the elite in Muslim Iberia was much praised by poets (see figures 5.7 and 5.8). Samuel the Nagid

Figure 5.7   Detail from a miniature in the Barcelona Haggadah. *Source*: British Library, Add MS 14761, fol. 26.

writes, "Put out your lamps! Use crystal cups for light./Away with singers! Bottles are better than lutes."[116] In Ibn Quzmān's poem mentioned above, he cries: "Ho! Clink the glasses with us!" and later in the poem: "Take your bottle, lift it high and empty it!"[117]

The sound of wine, its appearance, its warmth, and its promise of forgetfulness tempted the poets of the Middle Ages. In Ibn Quzmān's *zéjel* 96, the sound of drinking wine is achieved in onomatopoeia:

The wine in the glass is moving: pour, pour [s · ub, s · ub];
drinking it, the lips do: sip, sip ['ub, 'ub];
while the gorge, swallowing it, goes: gulp, gulp [dub, dub].[118]

Amilia Buturovic writes, "this onomatopoeia is just one of the successful sound reproductions Ibn Quzmān creates by using both the Romance and Arabic, confirming his mastery in achieving original aesthetic effects."[119]

Wine served to mark holidays, births, weddings, and funerals. Wine was used to confirm contracts, businesses, and bribes and was often used

Figure 5.8 **An Islamic glass goblet from the eighth or ninth century, probably made in Iraq or Syria (Abbasid or Umayyad periods).** *Source*: Metropolitan Museum of Art.

as payments for daily workers.[120] Upon his conquest of Ronda, the ruler of Seville al-Mu'tamid composed this verse:

Bebimos,
cuando los párpados de la noche
se lavaban el negro antimonio
con el rocío de la aurora
y era suave la brisa,
un vino añejo como el oro,
de color puro y delicado cuerpo.[121]

We drink,
when the black antimony of the night's eyelids
are washed with the dew of dawn,
when the breeze is soft,
an aged wine, like gold,
pure of color and delicate of body.

Wine was drunk by everyone, unless proscribed for health or religious reasons, and even those were often ignored. The quality of wine, like the quality of other foods discussed in this book, varied widely. The wealthy consumed fine wines, and the poor, base wines. Muhammad b. Ahmad Al-Wassa in his tenth-century *Libro del Brocado* writes:

> *En este terreno los elegantes, los hombres virtuosos y los hombres corteses, no beben vinos comunes, y sólo beben caldos más generosos, como el fermentado al sol, el de uvas pasa, el de miel, el arrope de uvas, el mosto concentrado. . . . Desdeñan el sirope de dátiles, pues es bebida del vulgo y de los plebeyos y lo beben tenderos y criados.*[122]
>
> ----
>
> In this land, elegant, virtuous, and courtly men do not drink common wines; they only drink wines that have fermented in the sun. They refuse wines made of raisins, honey, grape syrup, and must. . . . They disdain date wine, because it is the drink of the poor and only servants and shop keepers drink it.

Rodrigo-Estevan writes that Christians drinking with converts or Jews could be misinterpreted as an act against the Church.[123] The fear of wine as an element of idolatrous ritual prohibited Jewish consumption of wine produced by Christians. This prohibition, according to Freidenreich, carried a significant economic and social cost; economic because it hurt the wine trade between Jews and Christians, and social, because "Christians were deeply resentful of this Jewish practice."[124] Nevertheless, members of all three religions grew grapevines, produced wine, drank in taverns, held wine parties, and wrote copious verses about the virtues (and vices) of wine drinking. Overindulgence is condemned by all three religions as bad both for the body and for the soul. Medical professionals of all three religions agree on the medical benefits of wine, even those whose religion expressly forbids drinking.

The words of the Goliards ring true in the anthem *Gaudeamus Igitur*:

Let us live, then, and be glad
While young life's before us!
After youthful pastime had,
After old age hard and sad,
Earth will slumber o'er us.[125]

These lines hold the key to wine's general appeal. From dire warnings to jocular songs, the messages about the consumption of wine are mixed and, frankly, confusing. Christian texts would have us believe that wine served a sacred purpose and overindulgence leads to damnation. The Arab wine poetry that came out of the drinking parties contradicts the Qur'an's specific prohibition of all strong drink. In Judaism, drinking with members of other religions and cultures was prohibited, yet we have much evidence that demonstrates a true commensality. Although we may find a type of *convivencia* among the wine drinkers of medieval Iberia, the word itself has proven problematic and inaccurate. When considering the nature of wine drinking, however, we may be able to name it, rather, as conviviality rather than a coexistence.

NOTES

1. Susan Rose, *The Wine Trade in Medieval Europe 1000–1500* (London: Continuum International, 2011), 157.

2. Rose, *The Wine Trade*, 138.

3. Teresa de Castro Martínez, *El abastecimiento alimentario en el Reino de Granada (1482–1510)* (Granada: Editorial Universidad de Granada, 2004), 290.

4. Rose, *The Wine Trade*, 143.

5. Rose, *The Wine Trade*, 151–52.

6. Rose, *The Wine Trade*, 108.

7. Castro Martínez, *El abastecimiento alimentario*, 282.

8. Ana María Rivera Medina, *La civilización del viñedo en el primer Bilbao (1300–1600)* (Oleiras: Netbiblo, 2011), 116.

9. Rivera Medina, *La civilización*, 272.

10. Rivera Medina, *La civilización*, 273.

11. Castro Martínez, *El abastecimiento alimentario*, 292.

12. Thomas Glick, *Islamic and Christian Spain in the Early Middle Ages* (Leiden: Brill, 2005), 80.

13. Amira K. Bennison, "The Necklace of al-Shifā: 'Abbasid Borrowings in the Islamic West," *Oriens* 38 (2010): 254.

14. Bennison, "The Necklace of al-Shifā," 270.

15. David M. Freidenreich, *Foreigners and Their Food: Constructing Otherness in Jewish, Christian, and Islamic Law* (Berkeley: University of California Press, 2011), 62.

16. Teófilo Ruiz, *Crisis and Continuity: Land and Town in Late Medieval Castile* (Philadelphia: University of Pennsylvania Press, 1994), 82.

17. Ruiz, *Crisis and Continuity*, 80–81.

18. Ruiz, *Crisis and Continuity*, 81.

19. 'Abd al-Rahmān ibn Muhammad ibn Wāfid, *Tratado de agricultura*, trans. Cipriano Cuadrado Romero (Málaga: Analecta Malacitana, 1997), 92.

20. Ibn Wāfid, *Tratado de agricultura*, 95.

21. R. Dozy, ed., *Le Calendrier de Cordoue,* trans. Charles Pellat (Leiden: E.J. Brill, 1961), 28.

22. Dozy, *Le Calendrier*, 76, 88.

23. Dozy, *Le Calendrier*, 102.

24. Dozy, *Le Calendrier*, 118.

25. Juan de Aviñón, *Sevillana Medicina* (Sevilla: Enrique Rasco, 1885), 142.

26. Rose, *The Wine Trade*, 141.

27. Aviñon, *Sevillana Medicina*, 51.

28. Aviñon, *Sevillana Medicina*, 145–46.

29. Aviñon, *Sevillana Medicina*, 145.

30. Aviñon, *Sevillana Medicina*, 146.

31. Aviñon, *Sevillana Medicina*, 151.

32. Aviñon, *Sevillana Medicina*, 153–54.

33. Rose, *The Wine Trade*, 143.

34. David Waines, "Abu Zayd Al-Baklhī on the Nature of Forbidden Drink: A Medieval Islamic Controversy," in *Patterns of Everyday Life*, ed. David Waines (London: Routledge, 2002), 119.

35. Waines, "Abu Zayd Al-Baklhī," 113.

36. Waines, "Abu Zayd Al-Baklhī," 120.

37. Waines, "Abu Zayd Al-Baklhī," 114.

38. Waines, "Abu Zayd Al-Baklhī," 122.

39. Moses Maimonides, *Medical Aphorisms Treatises 1–5*, trans. Gerrit Bos (Salt Lake City: Brigham Young University Press, 2004), 69.

40. Maimonides, *Medical Aphorisms*, 71.

41. Benjamin Gersundheit, Reuven Or, Chanoch Gamliel, Fred Rosner, and Avraham Steinberg, "Treatment of Depression by Maimonides (1138–1204): Rabbi, Physician, and Philosopher," *American Journal of Psychiatry* 165, no. 4 (April 2008): 425.

42. Alicia Martínez Crespo, *Manual de mugeres en el qual se contienen muchas y diversas reçeutas muy buenas* (Salamanca: Universidad de Salamanca, 1995), 7–10.

43. Joan Santanach, ed., *The Book of Sent Soví: Medieval Recipes from Catalonia*, trans. Robin Vogelzang (Barcelona: Barcino-Tamesis, 2014), 145.

44. Santanach, *The Book of Sent Soví,* 53.

45. Santanach, *The Book of Sent Soví*, 187.

46. David M. Gitlitz and Linda Kay Davidson, *A Drizzle of Honey: The Lives and Recipes of Spain's Secret Jews* (New York: St. Martin's Press, 1999), 165.

47. Ibn Razīn al-Tugībī, *Relieves de las mesas, acerca de las delicias de la comida y los diferentes platos*, ed. and trans. Manuela Marín (Gijón: Ediciones Trea, S.L., 2007), 47.

48. Al-Tugībī, *Relieves de las mesas*, 47.

49. Al-Tugībī, *Relieves de las mesas*, 291–94.

50. Kevin R. Poole, "Sacrificio de la misa: The First Spanish Liturgical Textbook," *Hispania* 94, no. 1 (March 2011): 78.

51. Gonzalo de Berceo, *Milagros de Nuestra Señora*, ed. Michael Gerli (Madrid: Cátedra, 1988), 76, l. 39a.

52. Berceo, *Milagros*, 80, l. 55c.

53. Berceo, *Milagros*, 150, st. 463.

54. Gonzalo de Berceo, "The Miracles of Our Lady," in *The Collected Works of Gonzalo de Berceo*, trans. Jeannie K. Bartha, Annette Grant Cash, and Richard Terry Mount (Tempe: Arizona Center for Medieval and Renaissance Studies, 2008), 85, st. 463.

55. Pedro M. Pinero Ramírez, "In Taberna Quando Sumus: De Berceo al Lazarillo," in *Historia y cultura del vino en Andalucía*, ed. Juan José Iglesias Rodríguez (Seville, Spain: Universidad de Sevilla, 1995), 205.

56. Berceo, *Milagros*, 150, st. 466.

57. Berceo, "The Miracles," 85, st. 466.

58. Juan Ruiz, *The Book of Good Love*, trans. Elizabeth Drayson MacDonald, ed. Melveena McKendrick (London: Everyman, 1999), 134, st. 528.

59. Ruiz, *The Book of Good Love*, 135, st. 528.

60. Ruiz, *The Book of Good Love*, 138, st. 548.

61. Ruiz, *The Book of Good Love*, 139, st. 548.

62. Ruiz, *The Book of Good Love*, 274, ll. 1096cd.

63. Ruiz, *The Book of Good Love*, 275, ll. 1096cd.

64. Raymond P. Scheindlin, *Wine, Women and Death: Medieval Hebrew Poems on the Good Life* (Oxford: Oxford University Press, 1986), 6.

65. Scheindlin, *Wine, Women and Death*, 25–26.

66. Scheindlin, *Wine, Women and Death*, 28–30.

67. Judah Al-Harizi, *The Book of Tahkemoni: Jewish Tales from Medieval Spain*, trans. and ed. David Simha Segal (Portland: The Littman Library of Jewish Civilization, 2003), 551.

68. Al-Harizi, *The Book of Tahkemoni*, 237.

69. Al-Harizi, *The Book of Tahkemoni*, 236.

70. Al-Harizi, *The Book of Tahkemoni*, 237.

71. Scheindlin, *Wine, Women and Death*, 11.

72. Scheindlin, *Wine, Women and Death*, 51.

73. Scheindlin, *Wine, Women and Death*, 74.

74. Scheindlin, *Wine, Women and Death*, 43.

75. Scheindlin, *Wine, Women and Death*, 42.

76. Scheindlin, *Wine, Women and Death*, 65.

77. Scheindlin, *Wine, Women and Death*, 69.

78. Amilia Buturovic, "Ibn Quzmān," in *The Literature of Al-Andalus*, ed. Maria Rosa Menocal, Raymond P. Scheindlin, and Michael Sells (Cambridge: Cambridge University Press, 2012), 296.

79. Ibn Quzmān, *Cancionero andalusí*, ed. Federico Corriente (Madrid: Ediciones Hiperión, 1996), 52–53, 5.0–5.1.

80. Ibn Quzmān, *Cancionero andalusí*, 78, 11.0, 11.2.

81. James T. Monroe, *Hispano-Arabic Poetry: A Student Anthology* (Berkeley: University of California Press, 1974), 42–43.

82. Monroe, *Hispano-Arabic Poetry*, 260, 26.

83. Monroe, *Hispano-Arabic Poetry*, 43.

84. Quoted in Rose, *The Wine Trade*, 163.

85. Francesc Eiximenis, *Francesc Eiximenis: An Anthology*, trans. Robert D. Hughes (Barcelona: Barcino-Tamesis, 2008), 162.

86. Jorge J. E. Gracia, "Rules and Regulations for Drinking Wine in Francesc Eiximenis' 'Terç del Crestià' (1384)," *Traditio* 32 (1976): 380.

87. Gracia, "Rules and Regulations," 380.

88. Gonzalo de Berceo, "Del Sacrificio de la Misa," in *Obra Completa,* ed. B. Dutton et al. (Madrid: Espasa-Calpe, 1992), 969.

89. Gonzalo de Berceo, "The Sacrifice of the Mass," in *The Collected Works of Gonzalo de Berceo*, trans. Jeannie K. Bartha (Tempe: Arizona Center for Medieval and Renaissance Studies, 2008) 446.

90. Berceo, "Del Sacrificio de la Misa," 993.

91. Berceo, "The Sacrifice of the Mass," 446.

92. Berceo, "Del Sacrificio de la Misa," 967.

93. Berceo, "The Sacrifice of the Mass," 446.

94. Berceo, "Del Sacrificio de la Misa," 969, ll. 62ab.

95. Berceo, "The Sacrifice of the Mass," 446, ll. 62ab.

96. María Luz Rodrigo-Estevan, "El consumo de vino en el occidente medieval: Consideraciones socioculturales," in *La alimentación en la Corona de Aragón (siglos XIV–XV)*, ed. M. García Guatas, E. Piedrafita, and J. Barbacil (Zaragoza, España: Institución Fernando el Católico [C. S. I. C.], 2013), 108.

97. Susan Gray, "The Relationship between Theology and Praxis: The Issue of Transubstantiation in the Middle Ages," *QL* 95 (2014): 191.

98. Gray, "The Relationship between Theology and Praxis."

99. https://sourcebooks.fordham.edu/basis/lateran4.asp.

100. Poole, "Sacrificio de la misa," 8.

101. Quoted in Waines, "Abu Zayd Al-Baklhī," 118.

102. Waines, "Abu Zayd Al-Baklhī," 118.

103. https://corpus.quran.com/translation.jsp?chapter=5&verse=90.

104. https://corpus.quran.com/translation.jsp?chapter=5&verse=91.

105. Mona Siddiqui, *The Good Muslim* (Cambridge: Cambridge University Press, 2012), 93.

106. Siddiqui, *The Good Muslim*, 94.

107. https://corpus.quran.com/translation.jsp?chapter=16&verse=67.

108. Siddiqui, *The Good Muslim*, 96.

109. Waines, "Abu Zayd Al-Baklhī," 119–20.

110. Moses Maimonides, *Obras médicas I: El régimen de la salud. Tratado sobre la curación de las hemorroides*, trans. Lola Ferrer (Barcelona: Herder, 2016), 52.

111. Quoted in Michael Strassfeld, *A Book of Life* (New York: Schocken Books, 2002), 70.

112. www.sefaria.org/Eruvin.65b?lang=bi.

113. www.biblegateway.com/passage/?search=Psalm%20128%3A3&version=NIV.

114. www.biblegateway.com/passage/?search=genesis+49.11&version=NIV.

115. Strassfeld, *A Book of Life*, 71.

116. Scheindlin, *Wine, Women and Death*, 47.

117. Monroe, *Hispano-Arabic Poetry*, 260, 26, ll. 11, 28.

118. Quoted in Buturovic, "Ibn Quzmān," 300.

119. Buturovic, "Ibn Quzmān," 300.

120. Rodrigo-Estevan, "El consumo de vino," 118.

121. Quoted in Ieva Reklaityte, "Yo, ella, la copa, el vino blanco y la oscuridad": El placer del vino en al-Andalus," in *Alimentar la ciudad en la Edad Media*, ed. Beatriz Arízaga Bolumburu and Jesús Ángel Solózano Telechea (Logroño, España: Instituto de Estudios Riojanos, 2009), 537.

122. Quoted in Reklaityte, "Yo, ella, la copa," 539.

123. Rodrigo-Estevan, "El consumo de vino," 120.

124. Freidenreich, *Foreigners and Their Food*, 201.

125. www.bartleby.com/library/song/140.html.

Conclusion

The creation of a community often relied upon notions of consumption and abstention of certain foods. To belong to a community was to feel a certain amount of security, in times of uncertainty. Religious laws prohibited commensality throughout the Middle Ages. Religiously speaking, to break bread with a nonbeliever was tantamount to being infected by their heretical beliefs. Laws were created to prevent commensality and the exchange of goods and services among members of different faiths.

The law code compiled under Alfonso X in the mid-thirteenth century stated clearly that Christians should not eat or drink with Jews.[1] Although the *Partidas* were "notably tolerant" toward the Jews regarding their religious practices, there was little tolerance of social activities.[2] However, as Madera Allan points out, laws preventing commensality between Jews and non-Jews had existed well before the thirteenth century.[3]

In 1324, ordinances by the bishop of Calahorra ruled that Christians should not enter the houses of Jews or Muslims or eat their foods. A *fuero* of Madrid states: "The butcher who sells the meat of the Jews, *trifá* or other meats that are exclusive to them, shall pay twelve *maravedíes* and, if he does not have the money, he shall be hanged."[4] The constant reiteration of these rules demonstrates that Christians often conveniently forgot them.[5] By the early fifteenth century, Castilian laws were established maintaining that Muslims were forbidden from selling anything edible to Christians. Olivia Remie Constable notes that these prohibitions were especially pointed against olive oil, honey, and rice.[6]

According to Michael Harney, the Alfonsine *Partidas* represent a racializing agenda by justifying collective dominance and subordination.[7] Harney does point out that to discuss race in the Middle Ages, as we understand it, is to be guilty of anachronism. The modern meaning of race, according to

Corominas, as "defining membership in inclusive categories of persons" does not appear until the sixteenth century.[8] There is no doubt, however, that the systematic conflation of cultural and religious beliefs and its concomitant notions of impurity is given voice in the annals of the Inquisition, the Edict of Expulsion, anti-Semitic chronicles, and other texts of the fifteenth century.

Commensality is at the heart of Christianity. Yet in the later Middle Ages, Iberian Christians utilized the particularities of Jewish and Muslim food cultures in a rhetorical battle against those religions. Through the use of the rhetoric of impurity, particular foodstuffs became targeted as Christian or non-Christian—that is, acceptable or unacceptable for consumption. Implicit in this labeling was the association of gluttony and sexual immorality with commensality.[9]

Sexuality and food consumption were never more inextricably linked in medieval Christianity than during Lent. Indeed, since Christians saw Ramadan as similar to Lent, Muslims were often criticized for not refraining from sex during this holy time. The fifteenth-century Franciscan friar and preacher Alfonso de Espina wrote in his *Fortalitium fidei contra iudaeos, sarracenos et alios christianae fidei inimicos*:

> The Saracens say that this fast is a precept in order to restrain the vices of flesh, thus being the starting point for penance. But whoever acts fasting during the day and eating thrice or four times during the night and enjoying good meat, and the best fruits, and women, those do not weaken but rather strengthen flesh and rouse forbidden words and deeds.[10]

Gluttony and hedonism were two characteristics that Christians bestowed upon Muslims. Both imply a lack of seemliness and a lack of control over one's nature. Joly observes that the list of foods in the "gluttony" section of Alfonso Martínez de Toledo's *Corbacho* has been compared to the culinary catalog in *La Lozana andaluza*, seemingly conflating one's religion with one's morality.[11]

To be called gluttonous was a common insult against all those who did not follow a Christian diet. Andrés Bernáldez's justification for the expulsion of the Jews states: "In this manner, they were *gluttons and great drinkers,* who never lost the Judaic custom of eating victuals, with earthen jars of stewed meats, onion and garlic dishes, fried in oil."[12] Pedro Aznar Cardona's justification of the expulsion of the Moriscos reads similarly: "*Eran brutos en sus comidas, comiendo siempre en tierra (como quienes eran) sin mesa. . . . Comían cosas viles (que hasta en esto han padecido en esta vida por juyzio del cielo)*" (They ate like animals, eating on the ground without a table. . . . They ate vile things and therefore suffered God's wrath).[13] Along with the devaluation of dietary customs of Jews and Muslims comes an imperative to equate these customs with inferiority; immorality of consumption became conflated with the impurity of religious beliefs. Mary Douglas explains that food taboos are cultural expressions of the notions of purity and pollution in a particular society.[14] Memmi writes that "the obsession with purity arises from a fear of pollution and a vow to obviate it."[15]

Literary texts often expose the hypocrisies that exist in a society. The condemnation of Christian consumption of meat coming from Jewish butcher shops is dealt with humorously in *Libro de buen amor*. Upon escaping from his prison and his woefully meager diet, Lord Carnal hides in the Jewish quarter among the Jewish butchers knowing full well that no Christian would look for him there. If we look at cooking manuals even into the sixteenth century, we can see how Jewish and Muslim food preferences influenced Christian cooking. Nadeau writes:

> From the fictional primary sources of novels and plays in which the lower classes savor the same vegetable dishes as those recorded in the court manuals and cookbooks, we get a sense of some of the central tastes of Spanish cuisine. . . . (Aldonza's) description of her grandmother's kitchen stands as the nexus between the food habits of Jewish, Muslim, and Christian ethnicities, between elite and underprivileged communities, and across centuries.[16]

There is no question that certain foods, identified as too foreign, lost popularity in the sixteenth century. Remie Constable and Nadeau point out the case of couscous. Couscous, as mentioned earlier, became a marker of cuisine deemed "too Muslim." Taking into consideration Aldonza's list of foods, however, it is clear that the cultural manifestations of religion were not easily erased.

Greater still than authoritative rules about who could eat with whom are the dietary differences that contributed dramatically to the "othering" of the late Middle Ages. Before the systematic annihilation of cultural differences was dealt its final blow in the early seventeenth century with the expulsion of the *moriscos* by Phillip III, persecution and prosecution of people based on their diets aided the process of Christianizing medieval Iberia.

Fernández-Morera, in his book *The Myth of the Andalusian Paradise*, aims to restore Christians as the rightful inhabitants of medieval Iberia. By arguing that academics have tried to distort the Iberian Middle Ages with terms like diversity and tolerance, he "furthers an explicitly extreme right-wing and conservative Christian political and cultural agenda."[17] Nirenberg warns against this kind of essentializing or whitewashing of history: " When we turn to history—medieval or any other—in order to demonstrate the exemplary virtues of a given culture or religious tradition in comparison with another, we are often re-creating the dynamics we claim to be transcending."[18] The mythology of historical perfection, then, requires a dismantling of the other for its success. The creation of the mythology of a White, Christian

Middle Ages is the creation of a mind that "aspires to the image of a perfect nation."[19]

During the Middle Ages in Iberia, religious rules pertaining to diet were created, enforced, and, often, ignored. Before the fifteenth century, differences in daily consumption had more to do with class than religion. However, once the acculturation of tastes became politically dangerous, the rules of diet and consumption became an important part of religious rhetoric.

Separating oneself from another community can be done easily with foods that are marked as strange, exotic, or just plain disgusting. As discussed in chapter 3, the eggplant became a symbol of the religious other. Sancho Panza calls the fictional original author of *Don Quijote* (Cide Hamete) *Berenjena* (Eggplant). "Eggplant eaters" and "doughnut makers," although seemingly innocuous nicknames, were associations that ultimately carried great weight with the Holy Office of the Inquisition.

James Amelang writes that "religious assimilation was predicated on the elimination of cultural difference."[20] The most banal customs, like specific ways of cooking, are often the ones that are targeted by rhetoric. To dominate the other's mode of being is the goal of racism.[21] In the beginning of the sixteenth century, daily customs such as bathing, certain kinds of dress, the limiting of the use of Arabic, and prescribed slaughter of animals was prohibited.[22]

The rhetoric of food impurity has been used throughout history to marginalize and justify prejudice and hatred. In October 1901, white Southern observers erupted when President Theodore Roosevelt, his wife, and their young children dined with the African American educator Booker T. Washington.[23] In Ensley, Alabama, just outside Birmingham, the local newspapers accused the president of having "invited a nigger to eat with his family."[24] Another newspaper that Riser cites conflates a simple dinner with sexual intercourse by describing the president as a "miscegenationist."[25] In the twentieth-century South, one of the greatest "sins" that White people could commit was the act of "eating with Negroes."[26]

Like the rhetoric used against the Jews in the fifteenth century, white Southerners like Virginia Durr remarked that one could not eat with African Americans because "they were offensive, smelled bad, and were diseased."[27] If we look back at Bernáldez's description of the Jews, we can see the same rhetoric employed: "They themselves had the odor of the Jews because of the dishes and because of not being baptized."[28]

Much has been written lately about the use of medieval tropes in the white supremacist movement. Andrew Elliott writes,

> In this climate, the Middle Ages have become particularly fertile ground for the kinds of pseudo-scientific race theories espoused by white supremacist blogs

and far-right nationalist groups. . . . In their fantasy Middle Ages, the resistance of Islamic expansion by white European armies was brought about simply because of the natural supremacy of the white race.[29]

This kind of "Medievalism" (i.e., fantasies of a past that bear little resemblance to history) is common among modern racists. The Nazis were guilty of it, as are the KKK.[30] This appropriation of a fantastical past is part of the mythologization of a White, Christian supremacy in the United States. Memmi writes that "a future seen as a projection of the past is amalgamated with a past reconstructed as a function of the future."[31] The desire to return to an idealized past ties in with the duality of the purity/impurity rhetoric. Orianna Falacci, in a racist rant against Muslims, condemned them for, among other things, requiring their meat to be slaughtered in a "barbaric manner."[32] These same words were used by Aznar Cardona in the seventeenth century: "They didn't drink wine nor did they eat or buy meat that hadn't been killed according to the rite of Muhammed."[33]

Modern hate crimes have made use of a mythologized power of pig fat. There have been multiple reports of using pork products to vandalize mosques and synagogues in the United States and in Europe. Matthew Sedacca writes that these attacks "suggest that some in the West now view pork as not just a good insult, but an almost magic talisman that will somehow ward off scary Muslims who fear any contact with the stuff."[34]

Pork has been used as a weapon throughout history. Hermann Fechenbach, when writing about his Jewish family's experiences living in 1933 Germany during Hitler's rise to power, described how when the Nazis desecrated and ransacked synagogues, they sometimes would smear pork fat on the Holy Ark.[35] Seemingly ridiculous, the mythologization of the pork taboo has become part of the structural bias and racial hatred that has blossomed in the post-9/11 world. The idea of dipping bullets in pig fat to send Muslims straight to hell is a continuation of the racist rhetoric we see playing out in the fifteenth century in Iberia.

Supremacists rally around the pork issue as central to the difference between them and the Muslim and Jewish other. In *The Devil's Historians*, Kaufman and Sturtevant write: "Throughout the wars in Iraq and Afghanistan, some extremist Christian soldiers sported Crusades-themed patches meant to inflame their Muslim opponents: images of a medieval knight eating a pig's head that read 'PORK-EATING CRUSADER' in both English and Arabic."[36] Far-right Christian groups in France made certain that the soups made for the homeless were filled with pork products.[37] The Islamophobia that has swept Europe "conflates all Arabs under a religious designation." "Muslim immigrants today are the embodiment of the Moors of old."[38]

In Inquisitorial Spain, the conflation of cultural practices and religious beliefs became a stepping-stone to forced conversion and, ultimately, expulsion. Following a particular diet would mark one as moral or Christian, or immoral and non-Christian. Religious prohibitions of food and ritual food practices mark someone as "the other." In late medieval and early modern Spain, what you ate became who you were.

Purity of blood statutes worked toward narrowing an elite class of untainted Christians. But, as Anouar Majid writes, "we are all Moors," meaning that we are all of mixed race. We need to recognize our diverse past in order to "embrace the differences that enrich us all."[39] "Eres una de nosotros" (you are one of us), a woman told me one day in Seville when I revealed my Lebanese and Palestinian inheritance. I took that as the highest of compliments.

NOTES

1. "Las Siete Partidas: Laws on Jews, 1265," in *Medieval Sourcebook*, ed. Paul Halsall, partida VII, title XXIV, law VIII (Fordham University Center for Medieval Studies), accessed January 1, 2021, https://sourcebooks.fordham.edu/source/jews -sietepart.asp.

2. Ezequiel Borgognoni, "Los judíos en la legislación castellana medieval. Notas para su estudio (siglos X–XIII)," *Estudios de Historia de España* 14 (2012): 66.

3. Madera Allan, "Food Fight: Taste in the Inquisitorial Trials of Ciudad Real" (PhD dissertation, University of Pennsylvania, 2009), 27.

4. Isidro Bango, *Remembering Sepharad: Jewish Culture in Medieval Spain* (Madrid: State Corporation for Spanish Cultural Action Abroad, 2003), 47.

5. Borgognoni, "Los judíos en la legislación castellana medieval," 60.

6. Olivia Remie Constable, "Food and Meaning: Christian Understandings of Muslim Food and Food Ways in Spain, 1250–1550," *Viator* 44, no. 3 (2013): 208.

7. Michael Harney, *Race, Caste, and Indigeneity in Medieval Spanish Travel Literature* (London: Palgrave MacMillan, 2015), 55.

8. Harney, *Race, Caste, and Indigeneity*, 3.

9. David M. Freidenreich, *Foreigners and Their Food: Constructing Otherness in Jewish, Christian, and Islamic Law* (Berkeley: University of California Press, 2011), 97.

10. Ana Echevarría, "Food as a Custom among Spanish Muslims: From Islamic Sources to Inquisitorial Material," in *Essen und Fasten/Food and Fasting* (Cologne: Böhlau Verlag, 2017), 101.

11. Monique Joly, "A propósito del tema culinario en La lozana andaluza," *Journal of Hispanic Philology* 13, no. 2 (1989): 127–28.

12. David Raphael, *The Expulsion 1492 Chronicles* (North Hollywood: Carmi House Press, 1992), 63–64.

13. Quoted in Remie Constable, "Food and Meaning," 229.

14. Quoted in Muhammad Khalid Masud, "Food and the Notion of Purity in the Fatāwā Literature," in *La alimentación en las culturas Islámicas,* ed. Manuela Marín and David Waines (Madrid: Agencias Española de Cooperación Internacional, 1994), 90.

15. Albert Memmi, *Racism,* trans. Steve Martinot (Minneapolis: University of Minnesota Press, 2000), 67.

16. Carolyn A. Nadeau, *Food Matters: Alonso Quijano's Diet and the Discourse of Early Modern Spain* (Toronto: University of Toronto Press, 2016), 136.

17. S. J. Pearce, "The Myth of the Myth of the Andalusian Paradise: The Extreme Right and the American Revision of the History and Historiography of Medieval Spain," in *The Extreme Right and the Revision of History,* ed. Louie Dean Valencia-García (London: Routledge, 2020), 31.

18. David Nirenberg, "Sibling Rivalries, Scriptural Communities: What Medieval History Can and Cannot Teach Us about Relations between Judaism, Christianity, and Islam," in *Faithful Narratives,* ed. Nina Caputo and Andrea Sterk (Ithaca: Cornell University Press, 2014), 68.

19. Memmi, *Racism,* 65.

20. James Amelang, *Parallel Histories: Muslims and Jews in Inquisitorial Spain* (Baton Rouge: Louisiana State University Press, 2013), 15.

21. Memmi, *Racism,* 55.

22. Amelang, *Parallel Histories,* 16.

23. Robert Volney Riser II, "Prelude to the Movement: Disenfranchisement in Alabama's 1901 Constitution and the Anti-Disenfranchisement Cases" (PhD dissertation, University of Alabama, 2005), 398.

24. Riser, "Prelude to the Movement," 401.

25. Riser, "Prelude to the Movement," 402.

26. Angela Jill Cooley, "'Eating with Negroes': Food and Racial Taboo in the Twentieth-Century South," *The Southern Quarterly* 52, no. 2 (2015): 71.

27. Quoted in Cooley, "'Eating with Negroes,'" 73.

28. Raphael, *The Expulsion 1492 Chronicles,* 64.

29. Andrew Elliott, "A Vile Love Affair: Right Wing Nationalism and the Middle Ages," *The Public Medievalist,* February 14, 2017, www.publicmedievalist.com/vile-love-affair.

30. Josephine Livingston, "Racism, Medievalism, and the White Supremacists of Charlottesville," *New Republic,* August 15, 2017, newrepublic.com/article/144320/racism-medievalism-white-supremacists-charlottesville.

31. Memmi, *Racism,* 67.

32. Quoted in Anouar Majid, *We Are All Moors* (Minneapolis: University of Minnesota Press, 2009), 17n36.

33. Quoted in Remie Constable, "Food and Meaning," 229.

34. Matthew Sedacca, "The History of Food as a Weapon of Hate," *Eater,* January 20, 2016, www.eater.com/2016/1/20/10790614/bacon-mosque-hate-crime.

35. Hermann Fechenbach, "The Period of Nazi Persecution," accessed August 17, 2020, www.hermannfechenbach.com/nazi_persecution.html.

36. Amy S. Kaufman and Paul B. Sturtevant, *The Devil's Historians* (Toronto: University of Toronto Press, 2020), 139.

37. Majid, *We Are All Moors*, 167.

38. Majid, *We Are All Moors*, 154.

39. Majid, *We Are All Moors*, 176.

Bibliography

Alfonsi, Petrus. *Dialogue against the Jews*. Translated by Irven M. Resnick. Washington, DC: Catholic University of America Press, 2006.

———. *The Scholar's Guide*. Translated by Joseph Ramon Jones and John Esten Keller. Toronto: The Pontifical Institute of Mediaeval Studies, 1969.

Alfonso X, King. *Las Siete Partidas, Volume I*. Translated by Samuel Parsons Scott. Philadelphia: University of Pennsylvania Press, 2001.

Al-Harizi, Judah. *The Book of Tahkemoni: Jewish Tales from Medieval Spain*. Translated and edited by David Simha Segal. Portland: The Littman Library of Jewish Civilization, 2003.

Allan, Madera. "An Elusive Minimal Pair: Taste and Caste in Inquisitorial La Mancha." *Ehumanista* 25 (2013): 94–106.

———. "Food Fight: Taste in the Inquisitorial Trials of Ciudad Real." PhD dissertation, University of Pennsylvania, 2009.

Amelang, James. *Parallel Histories: Muslims and Jews in Inquisitorial Spain*. Baton Rouge: Louisiana State University Press, 2013.

Anderson, James. *Daily Life during the Spanish Inquisition*. Westport: Greenwood Press, 2002.

Aviñon, Juan de. *Sevillana Medicina*. Sevilla: Enrique Rasco, 1885.

Bango, Isidro. *Remembering Sepharad: Jewish Culture in Medieval Spain*. Madrid: State Corporation for Spanish Cultural Action Abroad, 2003.

Beinart, Haim. *Los conversos ante el Tribunal de la Inquisición*. Barcelona: Riopiedras Ediciones, 1983.

———. *Records of the Trials of the Spanish Inquisition in Ciudad Real, Volume One: The Trials of 1483–1485*. Jerusalem: The Israel Academy of Sciences and Humanities, 1974.

Bellón, Juan Alfredo. "Judíos y Conversos en el *Cancionero de Obras de Burlas Provocantes a Risa* (Valencia 1519)." *Miscelánea de estudios árabes y hebraicos*, no. 32 (1983): 133–49.

Bennison, Amira K. "The Necklace of al-Shifā: 'Abbasid Borrowings in the Islamic West." *Oriens* 38 (2010): 249–73.

Berceo, Gonzalo de. *The Collected Works of Gonzalo de Berceo.* Translated by Jeannie K. Bartha, Annette Grant Cash, and Richard Terry Mount. Tempe: Arizona Center for Medieval and Renaissance Studies, 2008.

———. *Milagros de Nuestra Señora.* Edited by Michael Gerli. Madrid: Ediciones Cátedra, 1988.

———. *Obra Completa.* Edited by Brian Dutton, Emilio Alarcos Llorach, Isabel Uría Maqua et al. Madrid: Espasa-Calpe, 1992.

Bernáldez, Andrés. *Historia de los Reyes Católicos Don Fernando y Doña Isabel.* Sevilla: Geofrin, 1870.

Bonnassie, Pierre, Pierre Guichard, and Marie Claude Gerbet. *Las Españas Medievales.* Translated by Bernat Hervas. Barcelona: Crítica Barcelona, 2001.

Borgognoni, Ezequiel. "Los judíos en la legislación castellana medieval. Notas para su estudio (siglos X–XIII)." *Estudios de Historia de España* 14 (2012): 53–68.

Bos, Gerrit, trans. *Maimonides on the regimen of health.* Leiden: Brill, 2019.

Buturovic, Amilia. "Ibn Quzmān." In *The Literature of Al-Andalus,* edited by Maria Rosa Menocal, Raymond P. Scheindlin, and Michael Sells, 292–305. Cambridge: Cambridge University Press, 2012.

Campbell, Jodi. *At the First Table: Food and Social Identity in Early Modern Spain.* Lincoln: University of Nebraska Press, 2017.

Castro Martínez, Teresa de. *El abastecimiento alimentario en el Reino de Granada (1482–1510).* Granada: Editorial Universidad de Granada, 2004.

———. "El gusto en la doctrina moral de la Iglesia en la Baja Edad Media." *Micrologus: Natura, Scienze e Società Medievali* (2002): 379–99.

Catlos, Brian. *Muslims of Medieval Latin Christendom, c. 1050–1614.* Cambridge: Cambridge University Press, 2014.

Cerrato Casado, Eduardo. "El Calendario de Córdoba como fuente para la reconstrucción de la topografía eclesiástica de la Córdoba." In *Nasara, extranjeros en su tierra: Estudios sobre cultura mozárabe y catálogo de exposición.* Córdoba: Cabildo Catedral de Córdoba, 2018.

Cole, Peter, ed. and trans. *The Dream of the Poem: Hebrew Poetry from Muslim and Christian Spain 950–1492.* Princeton: Princeton University Press, 2007.

Cooley, Angela Jill. "'Eating with Negroes': Food and Racial Taboo in the Twentieth-Century South." *The Southern Quarterly* 52, no. 2 (2015): 69–89.

Crespo, Antonio. "'Los Porceles de Murcia.' Comedia de Lope de Vega." *Revista Murgetana,* no. 109 (2003): 67–81.

Cruz Cruz, Juan, ed. *Dietética medieval: Apéndice con la versión castellana del regimen de salud de Arnaldo de Vilanova.* Huesca: La Val de Onsera, 1997.

Daas, Martha. "Food for the Soul: Feasting and Fasting in the Spanish Middle Ages." *eHumanista* 25 (2013): 65–74.

Douglas, Mary. "Deciphering a Meal." In *Food and Culture: A Reader,* edited by Carole M. Counihan and Penny Van Esterik, 36–54. London: Routledge, 1997.

———. *Purity and Danger.* New York: Frederick A. Praeger, 1966.

Dozy, R., ed. *Le Calendrier de Cordoue*. Translated by Charles Pellat. Leiden: E.J. Brill, 1961.

Duby, Georges. *Rural Economy and Country Life in the Medieval West*. Translated by Cynthia Postan. Philadelphia: University of Pennsylvania Press, 1998.

Echevarría, Ana. "Food as a Custom among Spanish Muslims: From Islamic Sources to Inquisitorial Material." In *Essen und Fasten/Food and Fasting*. Cologne: Böhlau Verlag, 2017.

Eiximenis, Francesc. *Francesc Eiximenis, An Anthology*. Translated by Robert D. Hughes. Barcelona: Barcino-Tamesis, 2008.

Elliott, Andrew. "A Vile Love Affair: Right Wing Nationalism and the Middle Ages." *The Public Medievalist,* February 14, 2017. www.publicmedievalist.com/vile-love -affair.

Epstein, Marc Michael. "Birds' Head Haggadah—Scholar Gives New Insights into Jewish Medieval Text." Medievalists.net, April 2012. www.medievalists.net/2012 /04/birds-head-haggadah-scholar-gives-new-insights-into-jewish-medieval-text.

Espadas Burgos, Manuel. "Aspectos sociorreligiosos de la alimentación española." *Hispania* 35, no. 131 (1975): 537–66.

Fábregas García, Adela. "El azúcar de caña en el mundo mediterráneo medieval." *Andalucía en la historia*, no. 45 (2014): 42–47.

Fabre-Vassas, Claudine. *The Singular Beast*. Translated by Carol Volk. New York: Columbia University Press, 1997.

Fechenbach, Hermann. "The Period of Nazi Persecution." Accessed August 17, 2020. www.hermannfechenbach.com/nazi_persecution.html.

Fernández Morera, Darío. *The Myth of the Andalusian Paradise*. Wilmington: ISI Books, 2016.

Freedman, Paul. *Out of the East*. New Haven: Yale University Press, 2008.

Freidenreich, David M. *Foreigners and Their Food: Constructing Otherness in Jewish, Christian, and Islamic Law*. Berkeley: University of California Press, 2011.

García Sánchez, Expiración. "El sabor de lo dulce en la gastronomía andalusí." In *La herencia árabe en la agricultura y el bienestar de Occidente*, edited by Fernando Nuez Viñals, 165–204. Valencia: Universidad Politécnica de Valencia, 2002.

———. "Especias y condimentos en la sociedad andalusí: Prácticas culinarias y aplicaciones dietéticas." In *El sabor del sabor: Hierbas aromáticas, condimentos y especias,* edited by Antonio Garrido Aranda, 71–96. Córdoba: Universidad de Córdoba, 2004.

———. "La alimentación de los andalusíes: Entre las normas médicas y la vida cotidiana." In *El Saber en al-Andalus. Textos y Estudios V: Homenaje a la profesora Dña. Carmen Ruiz Bravo-Villasante*, edited by Julia María Carabaza Bravo and Laila Carmen Mahmoud Makki Hornedo, 121–34. Sevilla: Editorial Universidad de Sevilla, 2011.

———. "La alimentación popular urbana en al-Andalus." *Arqueología medieval* 4 (1996): 219–36.

———. "Los cultivos de Al-Andalus y su influencia en la alimentación." Aragón vive su historia: Actas de las II Jornadas Internacionales de Cultura Islámica. *Teruel: Instituto Occidental de Cultura Islámica* (1988): 183–92.

Gázquez Ortiz, Antonio. *La cocina en tiempos del Arcipreste de Hita*. Madrid: Alianza Editorial, 2002.

Gersundheit, Benjamin, Reuven Or, Chanoch Gamliel, Fred Rosner, and Avraham Steinberg. "Treatment of Depression by Maimonides (1138–1204): Rabbi, Physician, and Philosopher." *American Journal of Psychiatry* 165, no. 4 (April 2008): 425–28.

Gil, Juan. "Los Berenjeneros: The Aubergine Eaters." In *The Conversos and Moriscos in Late Medieval Spain and Beyond, vol 1: Departures and Change*, edited by Kevin Ingram, 121–42. Leiden: Brill, 2009.

Gitlitz, David M. "Hybrid Conversos in the 'Libro Llamado el Alboraique.'" *Hispanic Review* 60 (1992): 1–17.

Gitlitz, David M., and Linda Kay Davidson. *A Drizzle of Honey: The Lives and Recipes of Spain's Secret Jews*. New York: St. Martin's Press, 1999.

Glick, Thomas. *Islamic and Christian Spain in the Early Middle Ages*. Leiden: Brill, 2005.

Gracia, Jorge J. E. "Rules and Regulations for Drinking Wine in Francesc Eiximenis' 'Terç del Crestià' (1384)." *Traditio* 32 (1976): 369–85.

Gray, Susan. "The Relationship between Theology and Praxis: The Issue of Transubstantiation in the Middle Ages." *QL* 95 (2014): 183–93.

Gybbon-Monypenny, G. B., ed. *Libro de buen amor*. Madrid: Clásicos Castalia, 1988.

Halsall, Paul, ed. *Internet Medieval Sourcebook*. Fordham University Center for Medieval Studies. Accessed January 1, 2021. https://sourcebooks.fordham.edu/basis/lateran4.asp.

Harney, Michael. *Race, Caste, and Indigeneity in Medieval Spanish Travel Literature*. London: Palgrave MacMillan, 2015.

Harvey, L. P. *Muslims in Spain, 1500–1614*. Chicago: University of Chicago Press, 1990.

Hea Kil, Sang. "A Diseased Body Politic." *Cultural Studies* 28, no. 2 (2014): 177–98.

Henisch, Bridget Ann. *Fast and Feast: Food in Medieval Society*. Philadelphia: Pennsylvania State University Press, 1976.

Hidalgo, Fernando, Jesús D. Lopez-Manjón, and Francisco Carrasco Fenech. "Cost Calculations, Religion, and Commerce: The Book of Good Government of the Souk of Málaga in the 13th Century." Seville: Universidad Pablo de Olavide, Department of Business Administration, Working Papers, 2009.

Ibn al-Khatīb. *Libro de cuidado de la salud durante las estaciones del año o Libro de higiene*. Translated by María de la Concepción Vazquez de Benito. Salamanca: Ediciones Universidad de Salamanca, 1984.

Ibn Quzmān. *Cancionero andalusí*. Edited by F. Corriente. Madrid: Hiperión, 1996.

Ibn Razīn al-Tugībī. *Relieves de las mesas, acerca de las delicias de la comida y los diferentes platos*. Edited and translated by Manuela Marín. Gijón, Spain: Ediciones Trea, S.L., 2007.

Ibn Wāfid, 'Abd al-Rahmān ibn Muhammad. *Tratado de agricultura*. Translated by Cipriano Cuadrado Romero. Málaga: Analecta Malacitana, 1997.

Ibn Zuhr, 'Abū-Marwān 'Abd al-Malik ibn Abī al-'Alā'. *Kitāb al-agdiya (Tratado de los alimentos)*. Edited by Expiración García Sánchez. Madrid: Consejo Superior de Investigaciones Científicas, 1992.

Izquierdo Benito, Ricardo. *Abastecimiento y alimentación en Toledo en el siglo XV.* Cuenca: Ediciones de la Universidad de Castilla-La Mancha, 2002.

Jewish Virtual Library: A Project of AICE. Accessed August 17, 2020. www.jewish virtuallibrary.org/vayikra-leviticus-chapter-11.

Joly, Monique. "A propósito del tema culinario en La lozana andaluza." *Journal of Hispanic Philology* 13, no. 2 (1989): 125–33.

Kaufman, Amy S., and Paul B. Sturtevant. *The Devil's Historians.* Toronto: University of Toronto Press, 2020.

Klemettilä, Hannele. *The Medieval Kitchen.* London: Reaktion Books Ltd., 2012.

Kritzeck, James. *Anthology of Islamic Literature: From the Rise of Islam to Modern Times.* New York: Holt, Rinehart, and Winston, 1964.

Kurtz, Barbara E. "'De la obra de la tienda de don Amor': Facetas de la alegoría del *Libro de buen amor*." *Romance Quarterly* 33, no. 2 (1986): 181–89.

Langley, Patricia. "Why a Pomegranate?" *BMJ: British Medical Journal* 321, no. 7269 (November 2000): 1153–54.

Léon Tello, Pilar. "Disposiciones sobre judíos en los fueros de Castilla y León." *Medievalia* 8 (1989): 223–52.

Livingston, Josephine. "Racism, Medievalism, and the White Supremacists of Charlottesville." *New Republic*, August 15, 2017. newrepublic.com/article/144320/raci sm-medievalism-white-supremacists-charlottesville.

Lobban, Richard A., Jr. "Pigs and Their Prohibition." *International Journal of Middle East Studies* 26, no. 1 (February 1994): 57–75.

López Quero, Salvador. "El léxico gastronómico medieval del Cancionero de Baena." *Zeitschrift für romanische Philologie* 127, no. 3 (2011): 476–502.

Maimonides, Moses. *Medical Aphorisms Treatises 1–5.* Translated by Gerrit Bos. Salt Lake City: Brigham Young University Press, 2004.

———. *Obras médicas I: El régimen de la salud. Tratado sobre la curación de las hemorroides.* Translated by Lola Ferrer. Barcelona: Herder, 2016.

Majid, Anouar. *We Are All Moors.* Minneapolis: University of Minnesota Press, 2009.

Martínez Crespo, Alicia, ed. *Manual de mugeres en el qual se contienen muchas y diversas reçeutas muy buenas.* Salamanca: Universidad de Salamanca, 1995.

Mártinez de Toledo, Alfonso. *Arcipreste de Talavera o Corbacho.* Edited by Michael Gerli. Madrid: Cátedra, 1998.

Martínez Kleiser, Luis. *Refranero general, ideológico español.* Madrid: Real Academia Española, 1953.

Masud, Muhammad Khalid. "Food and the Notion of Purity in the Fatāwā Literature." In *La alimentación en las culturas Islámicas,* edited by Manuela Marín and David Waines, 89–110. Madrid: Agencias Española de Cooperación Internacional, 1994.

Memmi, Albert. *Racism.* Translated by Steve Martinot. Minneapolis: University of Minnesota Press, 2000.

Mintz, Sidney. *Sweetness and Power.* New York: Viking Penguin, 1985.

Monroe, James T. *Hispano-Arabic Poetry: A Student Anthology.* Berkeley: University of California Press, 1974.

Montanari, Massimo. *Medieval Tastes.* New York: Columbia University Press, 2018.

Moore, John K., Jr. *Libro de los huéspedes (Escorial MS h.I.13): A Critical Edition.* Tempe: Arizona Center for Medieval and Renaissance Studies, 2008.

Mount, Richard Terry. "Levels of Meaning: Grains, Bread, and Bread Making as Informative Images in Berceo." *Hispania* 76, no. 1 (1993): 49–54.

Nadeau, Carolyn A. *Food Matters: Alonso Quijano's Diet and the Discourse of Early Modern Spain.* Toronto: University of Toronto Press, 2016.

Nichols, Stephen. "Seeing Food: An Anthropology of Ekphrasis, and Still Life in Classical and Medieval Examples." *MLN* 106 (1991): 818–51.

Nirenberg, David. "Figures of Thought and Figures of Flesh: 'Jews' and 'Judaism' in Late-Medieval Spanish Poetry and Politics." *Speculum* 81, no. 2 (2006): 398–426.

———. "Sibling Rivalries, Scriptural Communities: What Medieval History Can and Cannot Teach Us about Relations between Judaism, Christianity, and Islam." In *Faithful Narratives*, edited by Nina Caputo and Andrea Sterk, 63–79, 234–38. Ithaca: Cornell University Press, 2014.

Nola, Ruberto de. *Libro de cozina.* Barcelona: Paneuropea de Ediciones y Publicaciones, 1972.

O'Callaghan, Joseph. *A History of Medieval Spain.* Ithaca: Cornell University Press, 1983.

Pearce, S. J. "The Myth of *The Myth of the Andalusian Paradise*: The Extreme Right and the American Revision of the History and Historiography of Medieval Spain." In *The Extreme Right and the Revision of History*, edited by Louie Dean Valencia-García, 29–67. London: Routledge, 2020.

Pérès, Henri. *Esplendor de al-Andalus.* Translated by Mercedes García-Arenal. Madrid: Hiperión, 1953.

Pérez Vidal, José. *Medicina y dulcería en el Libro de buen amor.* Madrid: Cupsa Editorial, 1981.

Perry, Mary Elizabeth. "Between Muslim and Christian Worlds: Moriscas and Identity in Early Modern Spain." *The Muslim World* 95 (2005): 177–98.

Peters, Edward, trans. *The Edict of Expulsion.* Accessed August 17, 2020. www.sephardicstudies.org/decree.

Piedrafita Pérez, Elena. *La cocina de Aragón en la época medieval.* Zaragoza: Diputación de la Provincia de Zaragoza, 2012.

Pinero Ramírez, Pedro M. "In Taberna Quando Sumus: De Berceo al Lazarillo." In *Historia y cultura del vino en Andalucía*, edited by Juan José Iglesias Rodríguez, 201–20. Seville: Universidad de Sevilla, 1995.

Poole, Kevin R. "Sacrificio de la misa: The First Spanish Liturgical Textbook." *Hispania* 94, no. 1 (March 2011): 74–85.

Puñal Fernández, Tomás. *El Mercado en Madrid en la Baja Edad Media.* Madrid: Caja de Madrid, 1992.

Raphael, David. *The Expulsion 1492 Chronicles.* North Hollywood: Carmi House Press, 1992.

Real Academia Española. *Diccionario de la lengua Española.* Madrid: Real Academia Española 2001. www.rae.es/drae2001/hierba.

Reklaityte, Ieva. "Yo, ella, la copa, el vino blanco y la oscuridad": El placer del vino en al-Andalus." In *Alimentar la ciudad en la Edad Media*, edited by Beatriz Arízaga

Bolumburu and Jesús Ángel Solózano Telechea, 531–46. Logroño, España: Instituto de Estudios Riojanos, 2009.

Remie Constable, Olivia. "Food and Meaning: Christian Understandings of Muslim Food and Food Ways in Spain, 1250–1550." *Viator* 44, no. 3 (2013): 199–236.

Resnick, Irven. "Good Dog/Bad Dog: Dogs in Medieval Religious Polemics." *Enarratio* 18 (2013): 70–97.

———. "The Pig and Messianism in Medieval Jewish-Christian Polemics." In *Essen un Fasten/Food and Fasting,* edited by Dorothea Weltecke, 75–88. Cologne: Böhlau Verlag, 2017.

Riser, Robert Volney, II. "Prelude to the Movement: Disenfranchisement in Alabama's 1901 Constitution and the Anti-Disenfranchisement Cases." PhD dissertation, University of Alabama, 2005.

Rivera Medina, Ana María. *La civilización del viñedo en el primer Bilbao (1300–1600).* Oleiros: Netbiblo, 2011.

Rodrigo-Estevan, María Luz. "El consumo de vino en el occidente medieval: Consideraciones socioculturales." In *La alimentación en la Corona de Aragón (siglos XIV–XV),* edited by M. García Guatas, E. Piedrafita, and J. Barbacil, 101–33. Zaragoza, España: Institución Fernando el Católico (C. S. I. C.), 2013.

Rodríguez Puértolas, Julio. "Jews and Conversos in Fifteenth-Century Castilian Cancioneros: Texts and Contexts." In *Poetry at Court in Trastamaran Spain: From the Cancionero de Baena to the Cancionero general,* edited by E. Michael Gerli and Julian Weiss, 187–97. Tempe: Arizona Center for Medieval and Renaissance Studies, 1998.

Romero, Elena. "El olor del sábado: La adafina, del Arcipreste de Hita a las versiones 'light.'" In *La mesa puesta: Leyes, costumbres y recetas judías,* edited by Uriel Macías and Ricardo Izquierdo Benito, 215–40. Cuenca: Ediciones de la Universidad de Castilla-La Mancha, 2010.

Rose, Susan. *The Wine Trade in Medieval Europe 1000–1500.* London: Continuum International, 2011.

Rubiera Mata, María Jesús. "La dieta de Ibn Quzmān: Notas sobre la alimentación andalusí a través de su literatura." In *La alimentación en las culturas islámicas,* edited by Manuela Marín and David Waines, 127–36. Madrid: Agencia Española de Cooperación Internacional, 1994.

Rubin, Miri. *Gentile Tales: The Narrative Assault on Late Medieval Jews.* Yale University Press, 1999.

Ruiz, Juan. *The Book of Good Love.* Translated by Elizabeth Drayson MacDonald. Edited by Melveena McKendrick. London: Everyman, 1999.

Ruíz, Teófilo. *Crisis and Continuity: Land and Town in Late Medieval Castile.* Philadelphia: University of Pennsylvania Press, 1994.

Salas-Salvado, Jordi. "Diet and Dietetics in al-Andalus." *British Journal of Nutrition* 96, suppl. 1 (2006): s100–s104.

Sanchez, Galo. *El fuero de Madrid y los derechos locales castellanos.* Madrid: Ayuntamiento de Madrid, 1963.

Santanach, Joan, ed. *The Book of Sent Soví: Medieval Recipes from Catalonia*. Translated by Robin Vogelzang. Barcelona: Barcino-Tamesis, 2014.

Sato, Tsugitaka. *Sugar in the Social Life of Medieval Islam*. Leiden: Brill, 2015.

Scheindlin, Raymond P. *Wine, Women and Death: Medieval Hebrew Poems on the Good Life*. Oxford: Oxford University Press, 1986.

Scholberg, Kenneth. *Sátira e invectiva en la España medieval*. Madrid: Gredos, 1971.

Scully, Terence. *The Art of Cookery in the Middle Ages*. Woodbridge: The Boydell Press, 1995.

Sedacca, Matthew. "The History of Food as a Weapon of Hate." *Eater*, January 20, 2016. www.eater.com/2016/1/20/10790614/bacon-mosque-hate-crime.

Sefaria: A Living Library of Jewish Texts. Accessed November 9, 2020. www.sefaria.org/texts.

Siddiqui, Mona. *The Good Muslim*. Cambridge: Cambridge University Press, 2012.

Strassfeld, Michael. *A Book of Life*. New York: Schocken Books, 2002.

Suárez Fernández, Luis. *The Expulsion of the Jews: A European Problem*. Barcelona: Ariel, 2012.

Turner, Jack. *Spice*. New York: Knopf, 2004.

Usoz y Río, Luis de. *Cancionero de obras de burlas provocantes a risa*. Madrid, 1841.

Van Gelder, Geert Jan. *God's Banquet: Food in Classical Arabic Literature*. New York: Columbia University Press, 2000.

Vela, Carles. "Defining 'Apothecary' in the Medieval Crown of Aragon." In *Medieval Urban Identity: Health, Economy and Regulation,* edited by Flocel Sabaté, 127–42. Newcastle upon Tyne: Cambridge Scholars, 2015.

Vilanova, Arnaldo de. *Régimen de Salud*. Edited by Juan Cruz Cruz. Huesca: La Val de Onsera, 1997.

Vitale, Lisa. "Deprivation and Fullness: The Dietary Dialectics of St. Catherine of Siena." In *Table Talk: Perspectives on Food in Medieval Italian Literature*, edited by Christiana Purdy Moudarres, 53–69. Newcastle upon Tyne: Cambridge Scholars, 2010.

Waines, David. "Abu Zayd Al-Baklhī on the Nature of Forbidden Drink: A Medieval Islamic Controversy." In *Patterns of Everyday Life*, edited by David Waines, 329–44. London: Routledge, 2002.

Walker Bynum, Caroline. *Holy Feast and Holy Fast*. Berkeley: University of California Press, 1987.

Woolgar, C. M. "Food and Taste in Europe in the Middle Ages." In *Food: The History of Taste,* edited by Paul Freedman, 163–95. London: Thames & Hudson, 2007.

Zozaya Montes, Leonor. "Costumbres judaizantes femininas y transgesiones masculinas; análisis de las fuentes inquisitoriales en el tránsito de la Edad Media a la Moderna." *Investigaciones Feministas* 2 (2011): 355–77.

Index

Page numbers in italics represent figures.

153

About the Author

Dr. **Martha Daas** is an associate professor of medieval Spanish literature and chair of the Department of World Languages and Cultures at Old Dominion University. She has published on a number of Spanish texts including Berceo's *Milagros de Nuestra Señora*, the *Libro de buen amor*, and a variety of saints' tales. Her current research focuses on food in the Middle Ages and the cultures of consumption in medieval Iberia. She lives in Norfolk, Virginia.

9 781498 589598